The Glory of the English House

The Glory of the English House

Lionel Esher

PHOTOGRAPHS BY CLAY PERRY

BARRIE & JENKINS
LONDON

First published in Great Britain in 1991 by
Barrie & Jenkins Ltd
20 Vauxhall Bridge Road, London SW1V 2SA

Reprinted in 1997

ISBN 0 7529 0443 4

Designed by David Fordham

Typeset by SX Composing, Rayleigh, Essex
Reproduction by Colorlito, Milan
Printed and bound by Oriental Press, Dubai.

PAGE 1: A Tudor merchant's house in East Anglia. PAGE 2: A Grecian portico, West Wycombe. PAGE 5: A Georgian rectory in Dorset. PAGES 6-7: Longleat, a great house of the Renaissance. JACKET FRONT: Montacute House, Somerset; BACK: the Dougle Cube Room at Wilton House, Wiltshire.

Contents

Preface

THERE MUST BE WELL OVER FIFTEEN MILLION HOUSES IN England, and many thousands of them are attractive and interesting. To pick out a mere hundred can only be a very personal sample and one has to discipline oneself by certain rules, first of exclusion. I have excluded castles in the defensive sense (while admitting a few so entitled for romantic reasons). I have excluded the great palaces at one end of the scale of size and state-financed housing at the other. I have ruled out houses I cannot warm to, and in particular the kind of copyism that confuses the story and devalues the real thing, admitting only those whose designers, while taking inspiration from the past, had the wit to transform and transcend it.

In all my choices I have had Clay Perry in mind. Given two equal candidates, inclusion went to the more photogenic, and we even had to exclude one or two beauties (like Cotehele and Ightham Mote) because no static viewpoint conveys their quality, which is essentially kinetic. Finally, when in doubt, preference went to the unfamiliar.

The English care a great deal about the outside appearance of their houses, as you can see by the expensive and often regrettable refacing and refenestration of terrace houses and inter-war semi-detached ones when they change hands. But when it comes to visiting other people's – the houses that are open to the public – it is the other way round. Admitted by some side door or tradesmen's entrance, visitors seldom stand back to study the elevations to which the architect devoted so much thought and subtlety. It is the contents and bygone life-styles that fascinate, inauthentic though they often are. So this book concentates on the faces of houses, going inside only when the attraction is irresistible and the interior is an original part of an indivisible whole.

In studying the faces of houses we study the imagery, much of it unconscious, which caused them to change in each generation far more radically than can be accounted for by changing needs or techniques. This book is an attempt to let the reader see houses as they were designed to be seen, and enter into the minds of their designers.

Preamble

Round about the year 1800 Gabriel Wright, highly-skilled carpenter and joiner, lived in this house in the fast-developing village of Chelsea, just outside London.

His grandfather Thomas, of the same trade, had lived in a cottage like this in the Middlesex meadows, in the village of Ealing.

His grandson Albert lived in one of these, on the newly built-up slopes leading to Clapham Common.

Albert's grandson Cyril had a £500 mortgage on one of the new semi-detached houses along the Great West Road.

Today, the family having gone up in the world a notch or two, Cyril's grandson Kevin commutes from this half-timbered one in Shiplake, Oxfordshire, bought while they were still affordable.

All these small houses were built for the same needs with more or less the same technology, using bricks, plaster and bits of wood. Why do they all look so different? To answer this question, we need to explore the minds of the people who designed them.

CHAPTER 1

Messrs Carpenter, Mason & Thatcher

Great Chalfield Manor, Wiltshire

P EOPLE'S NEEDS AND WANTS (NOT THE SAME) DID OF COURSE vary with the condition of society and their own social status, and technology through the centuries did develop slowly, as we shall see; and even before the 'architect' appeared on the scene the human imagination, among those who had the leisure to indulge it, applied itself to the elegant silhouettes of castles and the miraculous structures of cathedrals. So it makes sense to drive a troika through the history of the English house, the horses being:

| NEEDS AND WANTS | TECHNOLOGIES | IMAGERY |

or, in Sir Henry Wotton's famous definition of 1624:

| 'COMMODITIE | FIRMENESS | DELIGHT' |

Outside the towns, none of which except London had a population of more than 10,000, we have to picture the medieval landscape as a patchwork of clearings out of the primeval forest. In the centre of each clearing, in a huddle of thatched hovels, lived the villeins and their animals, sharing their roofs. Out on the forest fringes camped the outcasts, tinkers, witches, casual labourers. And at the heart, in his wood-framed hall, close to the little church, lived the Lord of the Manor, the settler who got there first. Barns of that era have survived, but none of the free-standing wooden halls, probably because of the sparks that flew up from the fire in the centre of the straw-covered earth floor. The first need, after shelter, is for privacy – most simply met by adding a sleeping space, or withdrawing room, and another annexe for food preparation, to the communal hall. So the hall, as in any African village, develops into a cluster – a cluster of thatched sheds, since Britain is a rainy, tree-covered island.

PRECEDING PAGES *Central in the north front of moated Oxburgh Hall in Norfolk (1482) is a tall, twin-turreted gatehouse which became the model for Oxford and Cambridge colleges.* OPPOSITE: *Cothay in Somerset, an austere courtyard house of the 1480s, is entered through a battlemented gateway aligned with the doorway to the hall.*

Brewer Street Farm, at Bletchingley in Surrey, is unusually symmetrical for its date and timber-framed construction.

Having dined on the dais the lord and lady could retire to their sleeping quarters above the store-room. Behind the screen at the other end, guests withdrew through the porch on one side (recently added to reduce draughts), servants through the door on the other, which leads to kitchen and buttery. This is the making of the familiar H-shaped manor house with its central hall, increasingly elaborate timber roof, and asymmetrical wings on either side.

Soon there would be bedrooms upstairs in both wings, and a private 'solar' or drawing-room replaced the store-room behind the hall dais. All through the Middle Ages, and well into the 16th century, the only part of the manor house entered by visitors was the hall, so naturally such display and decoration as could be achieved was lavished on it. Arms and armour and hunting trophies would hang there, the walls down each side would be protected from lolling diners by oak panelling and the screen at the end offered opportunities for intricate carving. Finally, when glass could be afforded, a great mullioned window, perhaps with coloured coats of arms, would be built to light the dais. All this will be familiar to those who have seen the hall of an Oxford or Cambridge college, or visited one of the great Tudor houses.

As rooms increased in size and number and ceased to be the private retreats of the family, the hall lost its original role and became a formal vestibule, with doors symmetrically arranged to give access to other rooms and staircases. It acquired Classical grandeur, as the heart and concourse of the typical Georgian house. But later this grandeur was lost in the complex assemblage of Victorian reception rooms, and downgraded eventually to today's tiny lobby and home for that 1960s' symbol of domestic entrapment – the Pram in the Hall.

But for several centuries the hall dominated the house. The wooden farmhouses of Suffolk and Essex show the shape that emerged in the 15th century, with high-roofed hall in the centre and two-storey wings on either side. There is no attempt at symmetry, because symmetry runs against the carpenter's natural instinct to improvise: the shape of the piece determines the shape of the product. All the same, the H-shape was itself halfway to symmetry – another human instinct allied to the symmetry of our bodies (nothing to do with the influence of classical arthitecture). We find it in the elegant farmhouse at Bletchingley in Surrey, where it does feel somehow at odds with the natural informality of timber construction. This conflict between symmetry and asymmetry will be a recurring theme.

ABOVE *The hall of Stokesay Castle on the Welsh border (c. 1270) is simply a great barn with windows, here part boarded as they would originally have been. From the earth floor a rough stair led up to the solar in the tower.* OPPOSITE *Stokesay from the churchyard, with Tudor rooms bracketed off the top of medieval walls. Behind are the hall windows, with the tower beyond.*

Of course where there was stone beneath their feet or close by, men used it even for the most primitive buildings. Since it comes up in random chunks, the easiest way to build with it was in a circle: the sharp-edged right-angle would have meant a lot of arduous shaping. Lords in stone country would dig a ring of moat, pile up a platform inside it and run a roughly circular wall around the platform with a gatehouse on one side and the hall etc across the yard on the other.

Stokesay Castle in Shropshire is an incredibly picturesque example of the casual accretion, blissfully contemptuous of the right-angle, that gathered around the polygonal 12th-century keep that the lord had acquired in the 13th century. There is a rickety half-timbered gatehouse, another tower, an oversailing wood-framed top, a two-storey wing, and an enormous barn-like hall, with heavy A-shaped roof trusses, dated as early as 1270. All is proudly basic, with no fripperies. The picturesqueness is un-selfconscious here, though affection for the casual was before long to become an English addiction.

If Stokesay feels infinitely remote from us, how different are the many manor houses of the 15th century. For one thing, all defensive pretensions have been shed, although there are often still a moat (for a fishpond) and a gatehouse (for servants); for another, their size is admirably adapted

The main front of Cothay Manor, with the two tall hall windows, and the wings but-
tressed at their corners and generously windowed to suit the rooms themselves rather
than any notion of symmetry.

to our life-style, with the one big room for a party we all wish we had. Cothay in west Somerset is just such a house. It is not showy at all: the gatehouse is plain, the house itself equally so, with a smooth face of pinky-brown stone, corner buttresses, and generous windows. The hall is quite modest, with four tall windows high up and a wall fireplace. The whole H-shape is sensibly brought together under a single ridge. This is, I suppose, a Gothic house, but it is also an example of how, at the very time when in the rest of northern Europe Gothic had become more and more convoluted and elaborate, in England the Perpendicular style had almost reached stylelessness. Great Chalfield Manor, a house of the same

period lost among narrow lanes in a remote part of Wiltshire, is subtly dif-ferent and more obviously 'designed', with its separated roofs, carved finials on the gables, and two elegant oriel windows marking the two bedchambers. The close neighbourliness with the little church is characteristic.

Two things now transformed the late medieval scene. The first was sheep, which could more safely graze in this island than in the war-ravaged continent. (There are thought to have been 18 million of them in England in the 14th century.) The squire now needed fewer hands; he wanted money. It suited him to take rents rather than service. So the yeoman

The opposite is the case at Great Chalfield where, apart from the necessarily off-centre hall entrance, all is carefully symmetrical. Stables rise on the right, and the church appears on the left.

farmer emerged, escaped from the huddle around the village green, and built his own farmhouse on his own acres. The landowner, enriched by rents as well as wool sales, could afford to rebuild in dressed stone, and even to run to crenellations (largely decorative), if he could get a licence for them.

In the market towns, merchants, equally enriched, needed more storage space than their narrow two-storey gabled houses could give them. Confined on either side, they built upwards (still in oak), projecting each storey outwards in jetties to gain the extra strength which the cantilever gave them in the centre of the span. The effect is very picturesque to our eyes, but it was horribly combustible. The most specatacular jettied houses are in East Anglia, in Shrewsbury, and in York, where some have survived from 1320.

Jetty construction seems to have spread from the towns all over the countryside, where sometimes it was carried all round a building. Jetties had the additional advantage, in the days before gutters, of throwing rainwater well clear of the vulnerable plaster below. Wooden houses were prefabricated off site and could easily be taken apart, so that eventually, in New England as in England, it would be not uncommon, though sometimes regrettable, to remove them to new sites.

OPPOSITE *Ockwells Manor, built by an ambitious courtier in the prosperous Thames valley, boasts elaborately carved oak and a notable display of glass, then a luxury indicative of an owner's wealth.* ABOVE *Inside, the hall at Ockwells is timber-framed and panelled in oak, with heraldic glass showing the coats of arms of influential acquaintances and enriching a flood of light through the tall oriel window.*

The second transforming event was the arrival on the domestic scene of new materials – bricks and glass. Brickmaking had been a lost art in Britain since the Romans left, but now ships carrying wool out of east coast ports returned laden with Dutch bricks as ballast, and we gradually relearned the skill, first it seems on Humberside and then in East Anglia. We were then equally backward as glass-blowers, importing most of the glass for our churches. Whether in castle or cottage, the medieval British endured their climate without it, and small grey pieces only appeared in manor house windows in the late 15th century. Both bricks and glass were luxury materials available only to the rich for a century or more. The great

Elizabethan windows, rattling in the wind in their lead cames, were above all a display of wealth.

So, by the 15th century our needs and desires had assembled the materials and techniques which would see us through until the 19th. For the country squire, the merchant and the yeoman, wood remained the primary material; the ancestors of Gabriel Wright were the boldest and most ingenious carpenters in Europe. The London that burned so merrily in 1666 was a wooden city. It was this disaster, and the shortage of oak due partly to the growth of the navy, which finally established the ascendancy of brick in English urban building outside the limestone belt that runs

OPPOSITE *Gifford's Hall, a Suffolk wood-framed and moated manor house of 1480, is unusual in that the hall does not go up into the roof but supports an airy solar with splendid ceiling of its own.* ABOVE *Sparrowes house in Ipswich, an outstanding example of the pargetted plasterwork and oriel windows which were to be widely imitated in the 1870s.*

across the country from Gloucestershire to Northampton and the darker stone districts of the North.

But meanwhile the carpenters perfected their skills. If we leave Cothay and Great Chalfield and the limestone country and head east into the lower Thames Valley, what a transformation! Ockwells near Maidenhead is a frail lantern of delicate woodwork and glass, with red brick nogging filling the gaps in the oak framework. The H-plan is the same, the hall, porch and bay window roughly balancing one another, as do the two-storey wings. The house was built in 1465 by Sir John Norreys, who had profitably served both Henry VI and Edward IV, and this is manifestly no country squire's simple abode, but a courtier's show-place: the great hall window is gay with the coats of arms of his grander acquaintances. The contrast between it and the rather later Cothay foreshadows a theme which will counterpoint our whole story – the search of the fashionable for a new style versus the search of the more profound for an escape from style altogether.

Further east again, in East Anglia, the richest province of England, the use of wood is even more profuse, with the vertical studs close-spaced, then filled in with plaster, and it seems to have been a matter of indifference whether the whole was then plastered or not. In Suffolk villages like Clare and Kersey we can see both finishes, and in a beautiful wooden manor house like Giffords Hall at Wickhambrook, both in one building, contrasting and setting off one another, but both subject to the organic need of the wood frame to bend and twist. Here, the builders have greatly increased the importance of the upstairs rooms in the wings, having jettied structures to accommodate them. On the whole, in eastern England, the plaster covering was preferred, and if there was a pargeter in the village he would have a great time pattern-making like a child on a wet beach. This craft reached its peak in the 17th century with merchants' houses like Sparrowes (generally known as 'the Ancient House') in the centre of Ipswich, and was then lost until its revival late in the 19th century.

All these Lavenham (Suffolk) houses are framed in oak, as you can tell from its lively tendency to bend and twist. In some the framing is exposed, in others plastered over. Windows are later insertions. OPPOSITE *Paycocke, a clothier of Great Coggeshall in Essex, built his house in about 1500. Windows are random sized to suit the rooms, the oak brackets and beams are lovingly carved and the main doors have 'linenfold' panels.*

Of course the master woodworkers of the south east were not always so self-effacing. It was the era of the great church roofs, echoed on a scarcely smaller scale in some of the larger halls whose hammerbeam structures are one of the most brilliant inventions of the East Anglian carpenters. Externally the jettied beam ends might be elaborately carved, as in some of the Lavenham houses, or gabled bargeboards delicately fretted, as at Ockwells. Perhaps the prettiest of all the house fronts is Paycockes, a merchant's house of the early 16th century in the main street of Coggeshall in Essex, with slightly projected vertically mullioned windows, whose irregularities enhance the liveliness of the facade. Cornice and jetty beams are elaborately carved, as is the linenfold panelling of the carriage entrance. The pink brick nogging is a fairly recent insertion that, if anything, adds to the faded elegance of the whole. Eventually almost all of the houses of this period in the south east would be refaced in plain red brick, with the ubiquitous white sash window.

After the sophistication of Lavenham, Midland carpentry, as seen for example at Weobley in Herefordshire, can look pretty rough. And after the pale oak of the east the crude black and white of the west may be hard to take, partly because it has been so relentlessly yet feebly imitated since its resurrection in the 1870s. Nevertheless, one has to treat the western carpenters with respect. In Chester and Shrewsbury, exploiting the nature of framed construction, they had the courage to run their leaded windows straight across the house front from wall to wall, a feature not seen again for four centuries.

OPPOSITE *Little Moreton Hall in Cheshire was mainly built in the middle years of the 16th century, using wholly medieval carpentry technique. Upper stories lean and oversail in all directions, and at the top, in the roof, is a spectacular Long Gallery.* ABOVE *The Long Gallery at Little Moreton is glazed down both sides and was originally at both ends, exploiting framed construction in a way not seen again until the 20th century.*

NEXT PAGES *Pitchford Hall, here seen at dusk enfolded in its wooded valley, was built around 1570 by a wool merchant of Shrewsbury. It is E-shaped and almost symmetrical, with many chimneys, and gabled windows projected up through the eaves.*

At Little Moreton in Cheshire, one of the more extreme examples of pattern making in black and white, this long glazed strip runs close under the eaves, lighting a barn-like Long Gallery as flexed and creaky as a ship of the line. The grandest of the wooden manor houses of the western counties is Pitchford Hall, tucked away in a secret Shropshire valley and complete with the earliest tree house in England. Built by Adam Otley, mid-Elizabethan wool merchant of Shrewsbury, Pitchford is E-shaped, with long wings on the garden (originally entrance) side. As well as the wing gables, smaller ones break the eaves-line more or less symmetrically. Above is a forest of elegant brick chimneys, and the oak framing below is all functional yet decorated with diagonal bracing producing chevron and diamond patterns. Inside and out, the house is not only grand but cosy.

Most of our wooden houses were originally thatched, since this was not only the cheapest but also (despite appearances) the lightest of roofing materials. Reed thatch from the Norfolk marshes, the best of all, could last 60 years or more and was commonly used even for churches. Alec Clifton-Taylor notes that in Norfolk alone over 50 thatched churches have survived. More costly, but still cheaper than tiles in the stone belt, were the heavy limestone slates of Stonesfield in Oxfordshire and Collyweston, just outside Stamford in Lincolnshire, or the even heavier sandstones of the

Compton Wynyates in Warwickshire, perhaps the most romantically situated house in England, seen from its entrance gates on a frosty morning. It is a courtyard house of the 1520s, with a wide moat, and built entirely of many-coloured bricks. RIGHT *Also a courtier's house, and built over the same years, but on a more modest scale, Horeham Hall is one of the earliest brick houses in East Anglia. It has an exceptionally lofty hall window, and only pretends to be a castle.*

north. Of our wooden manor houses, Pitchford Hall and the farmhouse at Bletchingley are both roofed in local stone. Only in East Yorkshire were the dark stone houses refreshingly roofed in bright red pantiles brought from the Netherlands into the port of Hull. Conversely, Compton Wynyates, perhaps the most romantic house in England, which lies in the stone belt between Banbury and Warwick, is walled perversely and expensively in brick, but roofed in stone.

By the 1520s, when Compton Wynyates was built, English brickmaking was well into its stride. One of Henry VIII's courtiers rebuilt his wood-framed Essex manor house, Horeham, wholly in brick, but retained the traditional H-shape, with a grand oriel window to light his crenellated hall. Deliberately different wings and a turreted tower were added for fun.

His colleague, Sir William Compton, goes even further. Like Ightham Mote in Kent, Compton Wynyates is a courtyard house and was originally moated too; but whereas Ightham Mote has acquired its diversified character unaffectedly by accretion, and is ingeniously fitted together within its constraining square, Compton Wynyates is all projections and recessions, its intricacies enhanced by the lovely thin bricks in every shade from pale pink and orange to the purples that are used for the diaper patterns, then crowned by every variety of turret and chimney. The interior I remember from childhood as an infinity of rooms and staircases like a dream, with a threat, at dusk, of nightmare. Henry VIII used to stay in the house as a young man, while still married to Catherine of Aragon, and the vine-covered terraces which then climbed the steep slopes all around perhaps made her feel at home.

Completed in 1538, the originally symmetrical front of Hengrave Hall in Suffolk is built of stone with matching cream-coloured brickwork. Its central gateway is an elaboration of the Oxburgh theme, with pepperpot turrets and a delicately carved oriel window.

The courtyard house is a domestication and regularisation of the free-shaped medieval castle, and it was part of the pleasures of living in one to confront the world, across your moat, with a grandiose gate-house. The earliest and finest of them is at Oxburgh Hall in Norfolk (1482), north-facing, sombre and the centrepiece of a strictly symmetrical frontage. The low four-centred archway and the polygonal corner turrets were to become the model for Hampton Court, St James's, Lambeth, Eton, and the other colleges mainly built in the reigns of Henry VII and Henry VIII. Whether the hall at Oxburgh was placed to align its porch with the central axis we do not know, since it was demolished in 1778. This was never an easy problem to solve, since the great hall windows could not sensibly be matched on the opposite side of the entry. (It was easier in Oxford quadrangles, where hall and chapel could balance each other, as at Wadham, Oriel and St John's.) In complete contrast with grim Oxburgh is fantastical Hengrave Hall in Suffolk, another courtyard house with another unresolved central axis. This elaborate entry is self-consciously Gothic, even archaic, only the quite un-Gothic cherubs supporting the shields beneath the oriel window betraying that it dates from as late as 1538. Its pepperpot turrets were to be much enjoyed and imitated by Gothic Revivalists from Christopher Wren onwards.

One of the earliest of the great E-shaped houses is Barrington Court in Somerset, begun in 1514, in the local Ham Hill stone. The south front, while carefully symmetrical, is entirely medieval in detail, with barley-sugar chimneys and many crocketed pinnacles.

The courtyard house, while it survived until the triumph of the Palladians, was better adapted to Mediterranean climates than to more northern ones. Here it tended to be gloomy and denied Tudor designers the transparency and the blaze of daylight which they craved. So they returned to the H-plan, modified and greatly expanded it to the famous E-shape, and then carried it up to three or even four storeys, with central frontispiece, as it came to be called, and staircase towers in the internal angles. The flat back of the E made possible that characteristically English feature, the upstairs Long Gallery, where family portraits could be displayed and exercise taken on wet days. Barrington Court in Somerset (1514) is quietly Perpendicular in style and demonstrates that the symmetry of the E-shaped house owed nothing to Renaissance influences. Indeed nothing could be more Gothic than its spiky silhouette, with barley-sugar chimneys and pinnacles thrusting up from every gable and buttress. This passion for the vertical was to stretch happily into the next century and a half.

CHAPTER 2

The Tudor Renaissance

A vanished house of the 1660s, characteristic of its period and of its people.

THE FIRST E-SHAPED COUNTRY HOUSES, SO MUCH LARGER than any built hitherto, coincided with two pervasive changes in English society. The first was demographic. The population of England in 1500, at only 2¼ million, was still just one half of what it had been in the early 14th century, before the Black Death, the plague from the East which carried off one-third of the population of Europe in the late 1340s. Only around 1600, in England, did it at last recover to its medieval figure. This was a mixed blessing, leading as it did to wage depression, unemployment and vagrancy. But it enhanced the wealth of the territorial magnates on whom the Tudor sovereigns depended for their authority, and of course the size and elaboration of their houses.

The second pervasive change was the slow sunrise of the Renaissance. It was in 1414 that the manuscripts of Vitruvius' Ten Books on Architecture,

dated 50 BC, were discovered in the monastery of St Gallen. The central principle, which was in fact the central principle of all Renaissance art, is that Man is made in the image of God: the symmetry and proportions of his body must be reflected in the symmetry and proportions of buildings. The five classical Orders are then fully detailed.

That these strict rules were the origin and basis of the immense and romantic ruins of the Roman Empire among which they lived was a revelation to the Italians: they had cracked the code. As Palladio, writing in Venice in 1570, was to re-state it, 'beauty will result from the beautiful form and from the correspondence of the whole to the parts, of the parts between each other, and of these again to the whole; so that structures may appear an entire and complete body, wherein each member agrees with the other . . .'

OPPOSITE *Montacute House in Somerset.* PRECEDING PAGES *Sunset across the moat at Broughton. This great Oxfordshire house was begun in the 14th century, then improved and refaced in Tudor times, using the dark golden local ironstone. It has remained in the Fiennes family since 1451, scarcely altered since the reign of Elizabeth I.*

Longleat in Wiltshire, as it emerged in the 1570s in the final design by its owner Sir John Thynne: the first house to have matching façades on all four sides. OPPOSITE *In close-up one sees the three superimposed Orders, as used by Serlio in France, and the full-height projected bays, kept a few feet away from each corner to enhance the sculptural effect.*

Palladio did not merely say it: he did it. But before his time neither the Italians nor the French found classical design at all easy. The Romans themselves, after all, in a manner that would have shocked the Greeks (to whom the column was a load-bearing component only), applied the Orders as mere decoration to a great brick and concrete structure like the Colosseum, the pilasters supporting nothing. Early Renaissance architecture in Italy lacks all Roman *gravitas*, and when, after the invasion of Italy by Charles VIII, the French became aware of classical architecture and could hire its exponents, they too began by using the Orders as a language of ornament. (The same misunderstanding of Modernism was to occur in the 1930s in the decorative style now known as Art Deco.) Francis I's immense Chambord, so envied and admired by Henry VIII (whose one great architectural effort, the now vanished Nonsuch Palace, was a naive copy of it), was closer to the imagery of a medieval illuminated manuscript such as *Les Très Riches Heures du Duc de Berry* than it was to anything remotely Roman.

Henry did import and employ Italian (not French) sculptors and artisans, but then ruined his own endeavours by wrecking the monasteries. For the rest of his reign England was out of bounds to major figures from Catholic countries. Only with the Elizabethan settlement and the confidence it inspired did the wealthy – a new generation ennobled by Royal favour and enriched by monastic spoils – feel like building again. Their text-books by then were the Italian Serlio's Five Books on Architecture (1559) and John Shute's handier treatise on the Orders, published a few years later. He was the first Englishman to take up the subject.

Just down the road from Barrington, nestling at the foot of the conical, jungle-clad hill from which its golden stone is quarried, is Montacute. Built about 75 years later, there is no better example of the slowness of the sunrise, of the romantic conservatism of English architecture. The Phelips's were modest Somerset yeomen until Edward made his way to the Inns of Court, prospered mightily at the Bar, and became in due course a distinguished judge. At first glance the great E-shaped house he built in

his native village, immensely tall, is simply Barrington writ large. Only when we study it in detail do we notice that the four-centred arch has gone, the more important windows have classical architraves, there is a classical balustrade across the main front, and life-sized statues in classical niches below it. Only one change was made in its hisory, when in 1786 the fifth Edward Phelips to live at Montacute moved the entrance from the south front to the north and bought for it a handsome frontispiece from a demolished Elizabethan house in Dorset. This is in a transitional Gothic/Renaissance style more primitive than the rest of the house. The Long Gallery, upstairs in the west wing, with its elegant central oriel, is the longest of all the Elizabethan galleries, and the garden is one of the very few surviving Elizabethan *parterres*, with two graceful gazebos at the corners.

If Montacute is conservative, Longleat is revolutionary. Sir John Thynne had begun his house in 1547 during the Protectorate of his master, the Duke of Somerset. But 20 years later, after a disastrous fire, he decided to make a fresh start. This, too, did not satisfy him, and it was not until 1572, with the support of two dedicated and imaginative master masons, Robert Smythson and Alan Maynard, that the fourth and final facades were begun. Three things about Longleat were remarkable. It was the first square courtyard house to dispense with the showy ex-medieval gateway. It was the first to use its novel flat roof for pleasure purposes, with little domed supper houses no doubt inspired by the surrealist roofscapes of Chambord. And it was the first great house to make the square, earth-to-sky bow window the ordering feature of the design. Taking these windows close to each of the four corners, Thynne's design (it can only, in the end, be credited to him) ensures that the great square house is consistent on all sides. For the rest, we have the familiar mullion windows necessary to hold the frail leaded lights, and the three Orders fairly corrected applied to the three storeys all round, in a manner already used by Serlio himself at Ancy-le-Franc. Resting in its lovely saucer of landscape, Longleat is a 'cool' design, something the Elizabethans could not stay with for long.

LEFT *The sombre silhouette of Hardwick in Derbyshire, with its enormous areas of glass increasing as they rise. The only decoration, on all six square towers, is the cresting with its initials of its builder, Elizabeth Countess of Shrewsbury.* ABOVE *The High Great Chamber has a barbaric frieze 12 feet high above its tapestried walls. The floors throughout are rush-matted.*

It was Smythson's fate to serve a succession of architectural obsessives, and occasionally (as at Wollaton) he was forced to act out of character and collaborate in the creation of a monster. The most remarkable of all his masters was in fact a woman, the notorious Bess of Hardwick. This formidable lady made an immense fortune by marrying a succession of husbands of steadily increasing grandeur, who only briefly survived their marriages, having left her all their possessions. Finally, as Countess of Shrewsbury, she determined to leave her most prestigious property, Chatsworth, and build herself a great house at Hardwick on a steep wooded slope facing the sunset, alongside her family's modest manor house. She moved in in 1597, aged 77, and lived in the house for 11 years.

Hardwick is a house of contradictions. Smythson's geometry, based on superimposed squares, is as impeccable as at Longleat or Wollaton, but the final effect is disquieting. In stormy weather the six dark, box-like towers, interweaving as one moves around, present a frightening image, unmitigated by their filigree cresting featuring the initials of the lady. But in radiant sunlight the huge windows sparkle with a thousand facets. The entrance under a loggia is insignificant and passes straight into a hall entered end-on – the first such lay-out in England to survive and the forerunner of many others.* Never fail to go inside. The hall confronts you with an example of Elizabethan (one is tempted to write British) schizophrenia.

*Notably the Jacobean Charlton House at Greenwich, where a plan that must have been copied from Hardwick results in a far less dramatic building.

Three domed gazebos crown the warm brick walls of Doddington in Lincolnshire, an E-shaped house built in the last years of Elizabeth I in a manner reminiscent of Robert Smythson's work at Hardwick. OPPOSITE *The Long Gallery at Chastleton in Oxfordshire, high up under the roof, runs the entire length of the north side and is unusual (though not unique) in having a barrel-vaulted ceiling richly plastered in floral patterns.*

Ahead, carrying a gallery, is a cool and correct Roman Doric colonnade, then to your right the enormous Hardwick arms in wild 'Celtic' plaster-work, the two darkly painted stags bringing to mind legendary figures such as Herne the Hunter and the antlered mummers of primitive folk-dancing. Wide stone stairs, innocent of the heavy balustrading of the period, wander gently upwards into far sunlit spaces floored with rush-matting and walled with greenish tapestries – settings for *Hamlet* or *Twelfth Night*. The High Great Chamber is dominated by a 12ft-high plaster frieze of barbaric splendour – hunting scenes entwined with forest trees in high relief and painted. Beyond is the great Long Gallery, running the length of the garden front, flooded with light from its enormous windows, with two magnificent chimney-pieces and tapestries for which Bess paid a fortune, then covered with family portraits including those of three of her husbands. These magical rooms leave us with a softer image of Bess of Hardwick, not unworthy to take her place with Diane de Poitiers and Catherine de Medici, the creators of Anet and Chenonceaux.

So powerful is the image of Hardwick, so rectangular its geometry, that several other more modest houses with similar characteristics have been attributed to Robert Smythson. Five minutes away up the M1 motorway, swamped in industrial squalor, is Barlborough, tiny and forlorn on its high

The compact, huddled plan of Chastleton, like Hardwick's, is a composition of squares, but the windows here diminish upwards. The hall window in the right bay is artfully replicated on the left, with the entry tucked away in the shadows behind it.

podium at the end of a long lime avenue. Off to the east on the road to Lincoln is Doddington, not forlorn at all, but warmly welcoming, with its orange brickwork, uncompromisingly rectangular outline and three little roof gazebos reminiscent of Longleat. Hidden away in a remote enclave of North Oxfordshire is Chastleton, gabled for once, but equally close knit, with its cluster of square towers each rising dizzily from the centre of the four faces of a perfect square built around a little square court: geometry *in excelsis*. Up in the roof is a barrel-vaulted, richly plastered Long Gallery, a descendant of the medieval one at Little Moreton. Last in date (1611), and most romantic of all, is Wotton Lodge on the eastern edge of Stafford-

shire, a mere frontispiece really – one room deep – perched at the far edge of a natural promontory falling steeply away into forests and pools. Here the mix of square, angled and rounded bays gives a softer outline. The proportions are subtle and elegant, the charming doorcase and crowning balustrade the only adornments. It is a true culmination of Elizabethan architecture – in one sense.

For there are others. Wotton was a hunting lodge attached to a great house nearby, and the other Smythsonian houses including and following Hardwick were glorified, much glorified, manor houses at the heart of substantial estates. But Longleat had been a place fit for a queen, and

Wotton Lodge in Staffordshire, built in 1611 and attributed to Robert Smythson, is a
true culmination of Elizabethan architecture.

planned so that it might be available to Elizabeth on one of her summer progresses, whereby that cautious lady saved having to spend her own money on building. Few of the new rich were in that league, and of them one of the earliest was Sir Humphrey Stafford. His great house, Kirby, is contemporary with Longleat, but compared with Longleat's measured prose it speaks the language of poetry.

Much has been written about the Elizabethan imagination. The age was just remote enough from the Middle Ages to feel romantic about them. Knights still affected armour, ladies were courted in the troubadour style, and, just as much as in the France of that age, the English aristocracy still

dreamed of living in fairy-tale castles, except that, where the Renaissance French continued to build fat round bastions and pepper-pot slate roofs, the English continued to build moats, gatehouses, and great timbered-roofed halls. But they wished it all to be bright and gay like a medieval manuscript. Pleasing decay (in John Piper's phrase) was not in their line at all. As well as this the Elizabethans, as in their poetry, loved intricacy, ingenuity, puzzles, symbolism: they liked to plan houses in the shape of their initials, or to a scheme composed entirely of triangles.

How utterly remote this was from the severities of Palladio! Kirby demonstrates perfectly the extraordinary marriage of opposites that

In contrast to Longleat, the courtyard of this beautiful mid-Elizabethan ruin, Kirby Hall in Northamptonshire, has giant Ionic pilasters, with classical entablatures crowning the upper windows. OPPOSITE *Last of the 'prodigy houses', Blickling in Norfolk was designed by Robert Lyminge and completed in 1627. The house is approached across a perfectly scaled entrance court framed by buildings with Dutch gables.*

resulted. The layout is traditional, with a spacious courtyard entered centrally and a central porch ahead leading into the full-height hall on its right, whose tall windows are symmetrically replicated on the left. But instead of the old-style gatehouse we have first a pair of beautiful classic archways, then an elegant Renaissance colonnade, and then, instead of buttresses between the hall windows, we find giant Corinthian pilasters copied from those of Philibert de l'Orme at Anet and carried round the whole courtyard. The frontispiece over the hall porch is an indescribable concoction of Renaissance imagery, topped by a Dutch gable, supported by a string of enchanting Corinthian colonnettes.

Kirby is the only ruin in this book, and deliberately so. No hard Victorian restorations here, instead the poignant quality all ruins have – enhancing the sculptural qualities of architecture, inviting you in, all secrets long since blown away.

That Dutch gable at Kirby is a hint of what was to come. The Duke of Alva's persecution of Protestants during the 1570s in the Spanish Netherlands led to an influx of refugees, including the grandfather of Vanbrugh (*see Chapter 4*), and a group of architectural craftsmen and draughtsmen whose novelties the Tudor and Stuart grandees found it impossible to resist. German/Dutch Renaissance buildings had a strong streak of vulgarity,

*The south front of Felbrigg, no doubt influenced by its neighbour Blickling, is much
more modest in scale and was originally only one room deep. There are interesting
additions of the 1670s and 1750s.*

which emerges not only at Wollaton but even in the great palaces of the Cecils at Burghley and Hatfield, favourite summer residences of the Queen. The sombre personality of Lord Burghley and the lighter touch of Robert Lyminge, the master carpenter at Hatfield, seem to have mitigated this late 16th-century tendency to vulgar ostentation, although scarcely so in the courtyard at Burghley or in the great hall at Hatfield. After Burghley, the amazing succession of 'prodigy houses', as Sir John Summerson called them, are all in brick with stone dressings, all have wide-spread symmetrical plans, turrets, carefully organised ranks of chimneys, balustraded parapets, bow-windows, elaborate frontispieces, great halls, long galleries. Since I have to choose, it must be the most remote, Blickling (1616-27), the last work known to have been designed by Lyminge (now described as an architect). It suddenly materialises at the end of a perfectly-scaled forecourt as you wander a Norfolk lane – a work of subtle art, much more sophisticated than the rough magic of Kirby, and the culmination, in another sense, of the Elizabethan-Jacobean story.

The joint between the two reigns is invisible, as we can verify if we drive short distances from Blickling to three more modest Norfolk halls – all Jacobean in date, yet all wholly Elizabethan in character. The south front at Felbrigg, built at the same time, and in the same mode, as Blickling,

*Barningham Hall, close by, is a decade earlier and its elaborate gabled dormers give
it a fantastical Elizabethan air.*

may have been designed by Lyminge and erected by his team. We can see
how conservative it was if we turn the corner to the west wing, which was
added only 50 years later. Some neighbours were shocked by its uncompromisingly 'modern' manner (although it did have mullioned windows,
replaced by Georgian sashes in the 1750s). Kirstead, by contrast, is still in
the modest Tudor vernacular with huge windows and stepped gables. Barningham is something else again – eccentric, fantastical, with tall, lacy
two-storey dormers that could have been copied from the 1490s courtyard
elevation of the chateau at Josselin, in Brittany. Latest in date, and very
much in the Blickling tradition, is the stone manor house at Lilford near

Ardbourne in Northamptonshire, with its unusually tall and narrow windows and its spectacular array of 13 chimneys connected by arches. These,
a favourite device of Vanbrugh and his imitators, date from 1711.

South of the Thames, we shall find many more variations on these now
familiar 16th- and 17th-century themes. Bramshill's long and beautifully
proportioned garden front has two elegant little Italian loggias which will
be found again at Cranborne – a popular 17th-century amenity which
would be lost to the country house for the next two centuries. Another
pleasure which the Palladians would soon dismiss is the varied textures of
building materials. Loseley, of the 1560s, a great house near Guildford, is

Lilford Hall in Northamptonshire, a perfect Jacobean design of 1635, is built in the local limestone, which is the finest and most durable in England. The thirteen chimneys were added a century later in the manner of Vanbrugh. OPPOSITE *Hidden away on Otmoor, near Oxford, is Beckley Park, a moated house of the 1540s on a site said to have belonged to King Alfred in the 9th century.*

virtually without classical ornament. It is not even symmetrical, allowing the functions of the various components of the long north front to determine their proportions with a sure sense of balance, and is faced with rough Bargate stone relieved by white clunch dressings. Beckley Park near Oxford, by contrast, is built of warm dark-red bricks with black bricks in diamond patterns, the original texture unspoilt by Victorian restorers. Its site on remote Otmoor is of great antiquity, with the remains of three moats, and is said to have belonged to King Alfred in the ninth century. Built in the 1540s as a hunting lodge for the Lord Williams who founded the Grammar School at nearby Thame, the house has the same hunched

quality as the later Chastleton, with three tall gabled towers rising grandly at the back; but the scale is much smaller and more intimate.

Wiltshire and Dorset are the counties whose pale historic buildings, by some strange alchemy, are more beautifully textured by time than those of any others. Cranborne, an old hunting lodge rebuilt early in the reign of James I by Robert Cecil 1st Earl of Salisbury, is faced with soft creamy plaster, its romantic silhouette of twin towers, gables and tall chimneys, embosomed in a deep dell among enormous trees. Gabled Lake House of 1580, in the Avon Valley north of Salisbury, has the flint and Portland stone chequerboard walls which are a feature of that chalk region. The

OPPOSITE *A loggia at Cranborne, the Cecils' Dorset hunting lodge. Designed in an elegant 16th-century version of Doric, the loggia is a Jacobean amenity which disappeared from English architecture until the 19th-century.* ABOVE *Anderson, a lost and lonely manor house in Dorset, is a perfect composition. It is contemporary with Cranborne, but feels much more Elizabethan, with its plum-red banded brickwork and pale Portland stone.*

enchanted Anderson Manor (1622), to my eyes the most beautiful of the three, hidden away at the end of an ancient avenue inland from Poole, has dark red bricks with horizontal stripes of blue headers and dressings of Portland stone. The estate had belonged in the 15th century to the Turbervilles (Thomas Hardy's d'Urbervilles). John Tregonwell, the owner of the monastic estate of Milton Abbey, bought it to build a small house for his retirement, but was thrown out of it in the Civil War at the age of 80. However, he bought it back, and it remained in his family until the 20th century. The two flat gables, hexagonal centrepiece and two banks of four angled chimneys are perfectly organised in relation to one another.

This is architecture – without architects. Smythson and Lyminge appear in the history books, but these were promoted craftsmen on daily rates or piecework, capable of drawing neat 'plattes' or 'uprights', but incapable (in the age of Leonardo!) of using drawing as a means of recording ideas. It was no coincidence that the most original and imaginative Tudor and Jacobean houses were those built by the most original and imaginative owners, though in the great majority of cases – the middle-sized halls and manor houses – we do not even know that much about their designers.

CHAPTER 3

A Call to Order

Clarendon House in Piccadilly, London, by Roger Pratt (1664).

ON THE DAWN OF THE ELIZABETHAN RENAISSANCE, IN 1573, nine years after Shakespeare, there was born to a Welsh cloth worker in Smithfield, London, a boy baptised Inigo Jones. Like most of the great architects of the succeeding century, Jones started life as something else – in his case a 'picture-maker', though no pictures have survived to attest it. What we do have are his designs for the Masques with which the Court enlivened the long winter evenings in Whitehall. These drawings are of a liveliness quite new in English art, and made it an easy step from imagining scenery to imagining buildings. Since his patroness was no less a person than James I's queen, Anne of Denmark, such opportunities soon arose, first as Surveyor to Henry, Prince of Wales and later, from 1615, as Surveyor of the King's Works. But before this great appointment came his way, Inigo Jones had spent a vital and eye-opening

year and a half in the suite of the brilliant young Thomas Howard, Earl of Arundel, exploring the cities of Italy, meeting practising architects, and inspecting the masterpieces of Palladio – and, most assiduously of all, the ruins of ancient Rome – the first English architect, as far as we know, to set eyes on them.

For a person returning from this unique experience, current Jacobean architecture, 'the monstrous Baubles of our modern Barbarism' (as Chapman put it) was insupportable. The absolute imperative was that architecture henceforth be, in Jones' own words, 'solid, proportionable according to the rules, masculine, and unaffected'. And he took the rules literally as regulative down to the smallest detail of architrave, entablature, and keystone, projecting whole elevations on the module of one column's diameter. Soon after his return came the perfect opportunity for a demon-

PRECEDING PAGES *The Queen's House at Greenwich, designed in the same year as Blickling (1616), was the work of a young Court theatre designer called Inigo Jones, and dramatically demonstrated an architectural revolution which was never widely popular.* OPPOSITE *Eltham Lodge, near Greenwich, another prototype: the first Dutch-style house in England, with the first 'hipped' roof (1664).*

LEFT *A splendid hipped-roof house of the 1680s is Honington Hall in Warwickshire, built in the warm brick and ironstone of the region and ornamented by a row of Roman emperor busts in oval recesses.* ABOVE *This house of the 1630s in Lincoln's Inn Fields by Inigo Jones is the prototype of the London terrace house based on the classical Base/Order/Attic configuration.*

stration. Designed in the same year as Blickling, The Queen's house at Greenwich (or rather, originally, a pair of houses linked by a bridge across the Dover road) begun for Anne and completed for Henrietta Maria, was the single most revolutionary building ever seen in England – 'a serene and simple statement [in Summerson's words] that might as easily belong to 1816 as 1616'. To Jacobean contemporaries neither of these qualities had any appeal. It seemed to them cold and intellectual, just as the first Modern houses were to do 300 years later. Yet it contains, opening off its severely cubical hall (again a prototype) the first, the boldest and one of the most elegant cantilevered spiral staircases in England.

Inigo Jones was responsible for advising on the design of a great many houses, principally in London, both as the King's Surveyor and as Architect to other great estates. In both capacities he oversaw the fourth Earl of Bedford's arcaded development of Covent Garden, modelled on the Place des Vosges in Paris, and the first regularly planned square in London, then later (1638) for Lincoln's Inn Fields, where Lindsey House has miraculously survived, the first terraced houses in London, and the ancestors of a type that was to spread all over the English-speaking world. The house next door shows how a Palladian architect, Giacomo Leoni, was quite content to go along with this prototype a century later, when Inigo Jones had

The south front of Wilton House in Wiltshire was designed by a French architect in the Jones office in 1636, but the pretty doorcase has no Jonesian severity – it is almost Baroque. The wide window spacing is the making of the design.

become an almost mythical master. The myth, encouraged by his assistant and nephew-in-law, John Webb, has led to the attribution to Inigo Jones of a number of country house facades. Of these the only certainty, and the only survivor, is the great south front at Wilton, designed by a French assistant with the master at his elbow. This has an individuality and sophistication that transcends the coolly correct Palladianism of his London buildings, with a joyous central feature that is already Baroque. Notice how the corner pavilions hold together a design which would drift on inconsequentially without them. They were to be widely imitated by the later Palladians, notably at Croome in Worcestershire and Lydiard Tregoze in Cornwall.

Inigo Jones, like Smythson, liked to plan in squares, and then to project them upwards as cubes or double cubes. The best known of the double cubes, measuring 60ft by 30ft by 30ft high, is the centrepiece of Wilton itself, a late work in which the plaster enrichments, gold on white, and in particular the ornate chimney-piece, all designed to set off the family por-

traits by Van Dyck, have a large masculinity which seems to stretch back to the Jacobean and forward to the Baroque. The great coved ceiling, painted in *trompe l'oeil*, softens the crude geometry of the double cube.

Many years were to pass after the death of Inigo Jones, in the midst of the Civil War, before English domestic architecture would recapture such exuberance. For with the Civil War we reach the end of the two centuries in which, for the first time in history, in France and then in England, the building of great houses, rather than the noble architecture of temples, theatres and cathedrals, dominated the visual arts. In France, of course, they were seen as chateaux, long after they needed to be, but in England they were seen quite simply as houses, and would continue to be.

The general insecurity after 1645 brought an end to Elizabethan adventurism and encouraged a mood of conservatism to which the Jonesian high style did not appeal. For most people who dared to build at all it was back to bricks and gables, whether of the traditional Tudor shape or in the new curvaceous mode introduced from Holland, pioneered at Raynham Hall in

Raynham Hall in Norfolk was begun in 1622 by Sir Roger Townshend under mixed Jonesian and Dutch influence. It has all the charm often found in amateur architecture. NEXT PAGES Built in the 1650s on the site of a larger, moated Tudor house, little Groombridge Place in Kent originally had mullioned windows with leaded casements.

Norfolk as early as 1622. Certain details in the original design have led to the assertion, not uncommon in houses of the period, that Inigo had a hand in the overall design, but it seems more probable that Sir Roger Townshend and his foreman bricklayer worked it out together. The huge voutes of the gable ends are certainly reminiscent of Inigo Jones' rather naive pre-Fire designs for the west front of St Paul's Cathedral; they end in absurd little Ionic capitals supporting conventional pediments, a detail Pevsner considers quite un-Jonesian. Raynham is a serene and spacious design compared with little Kew Palace, built a decade later by a London merchant of Dutch origin and known originally as The Dutch House. This is an elaborate essay in moulded brickwork, including the gables, cornices, window surrounds, and originally the windows themselves, which were leaded casements set in brick mullions – not a stone to be seen anywhere. Brick gables like this were unique to the 1630s and were not to be seen again in London till the Cadogan Estate went Dutch in the 1870s.

It was around 1650 that the first of two practical innovations occurred which profoundly affected the looks of English houses. This was the hipped roof. As we have seen, the men who built the grander Elizabethan palaces from Longleat onwards, with their Renaissance aspirations, found a traditionally tiled roof laid at 50° an embarrassment, and could afford to substitute lead flats and so see their lacy balustrades against the sky. But for lesser men, to whom lead was unaffordable and gables manifestly unclassical, the hipped roof, which gave them a cornice and skyline level all around, was the perfect solution. One of the first to use it was the remote and romantic Ashdown, built by the 1st Earl of Craven for his lifelong and unlucky love, Elizabeth, sister of Charles I and Winter Queen of Bohemia. When she was able to return to England at the Restoration she was already ill, and died in his London house without ever seeing it. Craven completed it in her memory and died a bachelor at the age of 90. Ashdown stands alone, open to all the winds that blow, in a fold of the Berkshire Downs, amongst unfenced woodlands where one expects to hear the sad sound of a French horn at sunset.

Kew Palace, built by a London merchant of Dutch origin, is an essay in moulded brickwork (the windows are later) such as was not to be seen again in London until the 1870s. OPPOSITE *Remote Ashdown, lost in a fold of the Berkshire Downs, was built by Lord Craven for his lifelong and unlucky love, the Winter Queen of Bohemia. It survives untouched since their day.*

In perfect contrast to Ashdown, snugly enfolded in a wooded Kentish valley, is russet-brick, utterly English, Groombridge Place. It was built in traditional H-shape within the courtyard of a large medieval house, so that it sits well back from its wide square moat. Insead of a gatehouse, you enter between two handsome stone piers, characteristic of the 1660s, marking the bridge. As at Chastleton, the off centre front door (necessitated by the traditional shape and position of the hall) is cleverly concealed, this time by an elegant little loggia and portico.

At Ashdown, fortunately, the usual 16th-century mullioned windows with their leaded casements have survived. These were still widely in use in the reign of Queen Anne, as on the west front of Tintinhull, a fine stone elevation which most people would describe as Georgian. But by then they were already a survival, because in the 1680s the second practical innovation of the century had arrived in London and rapidly spread across England. This was the sash window. Many 17th-century houses, including Felbrigg and Raynham as well as Groombridge, were refenestrated forthwith, and this was not necessarily a disimprovement. It was not so easy to fit them into the larger and more random window openings of Elizabethan houses, but where it could be done (Burton Agnes, Melford, Stonor), it was done without hesitation.

*At Tintinhull in Somerset is one of the few late 17th-century houses to retain its
original mullioned windows, without which most people would date it much later.*

One of the first of the hipped-roofed houses, and one which unquestionably gained from the insertion of sash windows, is Eltham Lodge
in Kent on the eastern fringes of London. It was designed by Hugh May, a
royalist architect who had escaped to the Netherlands in company with
the painter Peter Lely during the exile of Charles II. The Dutch influence
on the design of this house is quite evident, and it remains the surviving
prototype of the Georgian country house which was to spread all over
England in the 18th century. Few would guess it was built as early as 1664.

A generation later, in the same Dutch manner, but in a landscape wildly
different from the middle class suburbia in which Eltham Lodge is now
engulfed, the sunbleached red and white house of Uppark rose on the
crest of the South Downs on the western borders of Sussex – perhaps the
first great house to be so situated. I first saw it 50 years ago on a blue and
white day, when you could run down the steps and on forever into infinite
space, with the distant sea shining beyond a pale succession of ridges
and woodlands. Inside, the whole house was flooded in sunlight – not
good for the 18th-century fabrics which Lady Meade-Featherstonehaugh,
widow of the Admiral, ceaselessly mended. The house had been in his
family since 1747, and seems to have had a tradition of high spirits.
Fifteen-year-old Emma Hart (later Lord Nelson's Lady Hamilton) danced

Uppark (c. 1690) stands high on the South Downs, its large windows filling it with sunlight. This is how it looked before the tragic fire of 1989 – and how it will look again, though no photograph can convey its bleached and windblown elegance.

on the dining table in the 1780s. In 1825 Sir Harry Featherstonehaugh, aged 70, married his 20-year-old dairymaid, educated her in France and at the age of 92 left her his entire estate. It was her younger sister who in 1880 engaged the mother of H.G. Wells as housekeeper. His childhood at Uppark sooms to have had its traditional effects on him. That its original architect was the tiresome and quarrelsome William Talman seems hard to believe.*

It must have been hard to live in an age dominated by religious fundamentalism on the one hand and mechanistic science on the other (both, to our minds, fundamentally flawed). The confusion is made manifest in the

architecture of the period, in which the modernism of the day, represented by the brilliance of Sir Christopher Wren, had to contend with the nervousness and natural conservatism of an insecure age. When London burned down in 1666, at a time when in Paris Le Nôtre was aiming his perspectives at the western horizon, the citizens insisted on rebuilding on the medieval street pattern, and out in the provinces the Elizabethan E-shape, complete with diapered brickwork and mullioned windows, died

*The fire of 1989 which reduced Uppark to a shell has not, owing to the courage of the National Trust, led to the total demolition which followed the similar disaster at Coleshill. The salvaged furniture and fabrics will be returning to the rebuilt house.

ABOVE *Sudbury Hall in Derbyshire, begun in 1613, by the time of its completion in the 1670s had been updated by fashionable craftsmen from London.* OPPOSITE *The magnificent Long Gallery at Sudbury.* NEXT PAGES *Basically Tudor, The Vyne in Hampshire has the first classical portico in England (John Webb, 1655), Victorian battlements, Georgian windows and an elaborate staircase of the 1760s.*

hard. An extraordinary example of the transitional nature of the period is Sudbury Hall in Derbyshire, completed some years after Eltham. The Vernon family had owned the estate since 1513 and the squire who completed the Hall held it for 43 years from 1659. Externally, despite the hipped roof and cupola, the general character of the house, with its great chimneys, diapered brickwork, mullioned windows and elaborate frontispiece, is completely Jacobean. But the frontispiece itself is clearly of the Restoration, in the Baroque manner familiar to those who know Oxford, and it leads us into an interior to which the label Jacobean could never be applied. For his reception rooms George Vernon hired the most fashionable craftsmen from London – Edward Pierce for the magnificent staircase balustrade, the young Grinling Gibbons for the Drawing Room overmantel (a foretaste of his magnificent room at Petworth), and Robert Bradbury for the great ceiling of the Long Gallery which occupies the whole of the garden frontage. In the leap it makes from the age of Lyminge to the age of Wren, Inigo Jones might never have lived.

In fact 'Inigo's man', John Webb, soldiered on in Whitehall through the Commonwealth and into the Restoration, eventually to be eclipsed by the rising star of Wren. His most attractive achievement remains the plain but perfectly scaled portico attached to the garden front of a great Elizabethan house in Hampshire, The Vyne, in 1654 – the first such portico to appear on any English house.

Because he had been the first to use them in London, it became customary in the 18th century to accredit to Inigo Jones any country house of appropriate date with a string of giant pilasters across its front. The most spectacular example is Lees Court in Kent (1655), rebuilt after a fire in 1910. This has a giant Order 13 bays long. The design for the peculiar Ionic capitals (certainly not Palladian but possibly Serlian) could surely never have been submitted to the master, but the deep bracketted cornice is no more eccentric than that of St Paul's, Covent Garden, and might have been derived from it; there is, however, no evidence.

Jonesian influence, but nothing more, since it was built 26 years after

OPPOSITE *Thirteen bays long, the extraordinary design of Lees Court in Kent has been attributed to Inigo Jones. It has giant and crude Ionic pilasters and uniquely deep eaves carried on timber brackets.* ABOVE *The south front of Brympton d'Evercy in Somerset is equally eccentric – ten bays long, so that it has no central bay.*

his death, can also be seen in the long south front of Brympton d'Evercy near Yeovil in Somerset, with its alternating rounded and pointed architraves, as in the Whitehall Banqueting House. It is a delightfully dotty design, chopped off for no reason after the tenth bay, so that the elevation has a central hinge like a book (marked by a rainwater pipe). But who cares? This is one of the loveliest manor houses in England, with its Tudor front to which a graceful Georgian gothic porch like a lantern is attached, its clock-tower, vineyard, duck-pond, priest-house, and perfect little 14th-century church untouched by the Victorians, and all built in the golden stone of south Somerset.

The second half of the 17th century and Brympton d'Evercy itself is an appropriate time and place to note that it is this accretion of the centuries, this happy conjunction of styles, which is the charm of so many country houses and the natural expression of the chequered histories of the families which built them. Architectural historians tend to concentrate on the best and purest examples, when often it is their opposite we most enjoy.

The Vyne itself is a case in point. Nothing about its broad Elizabethan entrance front prepares one for the lakeside view to which the Henry VII Chapel, the Webb portico, the Georgian windows, and the battlements, give an ambivalence far more intriguing than 16th-century consistency – nor, come to that, for the equally variegated interior, with a miniature, rather congested, Palladian entrance hall and staircase inserted by the mid 18th-century Chaloner Chute, an architectural amateur who was a close friend of Horace Walpole.

The same, on a more modest scale, goes for Boughton Monchelsea. This handsome, remote house is unusual among its Elizabethan contemporaries in standing on a hill-top, commanding a panorama of the Kentish Weald. The garden front, facing the view, built in the local ragstone, is dated 1567, but was refenestrated in the 18th century and crenellated in the early 19th, and the broad expanse of wall is a welcome relaxation among the often over-glazed houses of the period.

But my favourite among all the many mixed-date houses is Compton

Boughton Monchelsea is unusual among Elizabethan houses in being built on a high hilltop, overlooking the Weald of Kent. The predominence of wall over (later) windows is also a rarity in houses of its period.

Beauchamp, secretly ensconced below the great Iron Age White Horse in Oxfordshire. The approach is completely French – lime avenue, classic stone front (1710) in the manner of Mansard, mossy fountain as might be in Aix-en-Provence; then cross the moat and enter a courtyard, with Elizabethan sides and a late 17th-century facade ahead. On again, and one emerges on to a spacious lawn bounded by enormously tall trees, and there behind one is a warm brick frontage, Elizabethan, entirely English. The house seems not only mixed date but mixed nationality.

Linear time has little relevance to such experiences, but we must in duty return to it. There is a missing link in the Restoration period,

represented by two great houses, both, alas!, now vanished. The first was Coleshill in North Oxfordshire (1650-60), destroyed by fire in 1952, the second Clarendon House in London's Piccadilly (1664), which survived for only 20 years. Both were the work of an amateur architect, Sir Roger Pratt, who had spent the period of the Civil War exploring classical architecture on the Continent and later produced such useful manuals as *Rules for the Guidance of Architects* and *Notes on the Building of Country Houses*, recommending owners to 'get some ingenious gentleman who has been somewhat versed in the best author of architecture viz Palladio, Scamozzi, Serlio etc to do it for you, and to give you a design for

RIGHT AND BELOW *The two contrasting fronts of Compton Beauchamp, which lies below the Iron Age White Horse in Oxfordshire. The north front of 1710, approached by a lime avenue, is almost a* Petit Trianon; *the south of 1600 is completely English.*

NEXT PAGES *Belton House in Lincolnshire, begun in 1685, is a more compact version (with Georgian windows) of London's vanished Clarendon House. It is built of superb Ancaster stone quarried nearby.*

Known to have been overseen by Christopher Wren, Winslow Hall near Buckingham
is massive and austere, with a sharpish pediment replicated on the garden side, and
enormous chimneys.

it on paper' – a role gentlemen were happy to play all through the following century.

Coleshill may well have had the help of Jones and Webb, but Clarendon House was the work of Sir Roger. Its design is beautifully imitated for us by Belton House, built by craftsmen for Sir John Brownlow around 1690. This great symmetrical house in Ancaster stone is still H-plan, but with hipped roof, balustraded platform above (known in New England as a Captain's Walk), and central cupola as at Ashdown. Clarendon House was to be the model for other late 17th-century houses all over England, generally more modest in scale. None is more attractive than Honington in Warwickshire, with its richly warm brickwork, elegant doorcase, and oval niches with Roman Emperors above the ground floor windows.

Houses like Eltham and Uppark are often described as Wrenish, and around 1700 it became common (as it had been with Inigo Jones) to claim Wren's authorship of red brick pedimented houses of their kind. In fact, despite his enormous prestige and his achievements in other fields, only one surviving house was almost certainly built under his eye. This is Winslow Hall in Buckinghamshire, built in 1700 for the Secretary to the Treasury, who had easy access to the great man. This is a tall, rather austere brick box, finely scaled, with a rather sharper than usual pediment to

A mason's house in the Cotswold vernacular in the main street of Mickleton in Gloucestshire, built in the last years of the 17th century. Its 'modern' features and excellent ironstone walling mark it as the work of an enterprising craftsman.

conform with the pitch of the hipped roof, and a positively Elizabethan array of monumental chimneys. If Winslow represents the architectural mainstream at the turn of the century, then Medford House, in the village street of Mickleton in Gloucestershire, is a nice backwater example, at a distance Jacobean, and only as you come closer manifestly much later. The beautifully porportioned golden stone front, with its Baroque doorcase and tiny *oeil-de-boeuf* windows looks too good to be a craftman's design, but it probably was. The Cotswolds, architecturally conservative to this day, are full of simple and timeless small manor houses, often built a lot later than you would think.

CHAPTER 4

Van's Genius

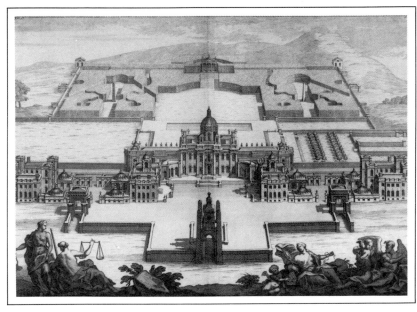

Castle Howard, the first great house of the 18th century.

F OR IN THE YEAR 1700 THINGS WERE HAPPENING WHICH WERE TO consign not just Medford but Winslow too, and even Belton, with all their progeny, to a respectable but out-of-touch old age. The foundations were going in for Castle Howard.

> Van's genius, without thought or lecture,
> Is hugely turn'd to architecture.*

John Vanbrugh was 36 – a successful playwright whose recent satirical piece, *The Provok'd Wife*, witty and accurate, had achieved a *succès de scandale* at Drury Lane three years earlier. His first play had been sketched in, of all places, the Bastille, where as a young soldier he had been imprisoned as a spy not long before – in conditions of considerable comfort** as well as

boredom. It was his plays as much as his adventures in Paris that brought him the company and friendship of the young Whig aristocracy in London, among them Charles Howard, Earl of Carlisle, five years younger than himself and set on building a great new house on his family estate in the hills north-east of York. The obvious answer, briefly attempted, was to go to the reputable William Talman, whose facades at Chatsworth he had recently admired. Instead, to everyone's amusement, Carlisle invited his friend Vanbrugh to design it, no doubt to the delight of old Wren, now 68 and mindful of his own late conversion to architecture. Wren even offered

---

*Dean Swift
**'Dinner', according to Sacheverell Sitwell, 'might consist of soup, fish, entrée, sweet, dessert and a couple of bottles of Burgundy to wash it down.'

PRECEDING PAGES *The spoils of office: Sir Robert Walpole's Houghton in Norfolk, a great Whig mansion of the 1720s.* OPPOSITE *The entrance forecourt and the central block of Castle Howard show Vanbrugh's powerfully sculpted massing, his interest in the skyline and his addiction to the use of rusticated masonry.*

The garden front of Castle Howard is like a great Baroque orangery – a complete change in atmosphere after the solemnity of the entrance forecourt. RIGHT *On the central axis to the south is this hyperactive Victorian fountain, with Atlas supporting the globe.*

Vanbrugh the services of his invaluable, discreet, and highly experienced assistant Nicholas Hawksmoor – a close collaboration which was to have the grandest consequences and lead to interminable who-did-what argument among scholars.

Castle Howard is rare among classical houses in not being sited for two axial viewpoints, back and front, but to be seen from all points of the compass and from considerable distances across the rolling Howardian Hills. For a detailed description the reader should refer to Pevsner,* who draws particular attention to the difference in character between the suite of state rooms on the 'festive' south side, mainly one storey like a great German Baroque orangery, and the 'sombre' north side, powerfully sculptural, ingeniously articulated, and prophetic of the more severe compositions of Vanbrugh's later years, as indeed is the lofty Great Hall beneath the dome, which has the feel of a smallish, dark, 17th-century church in the heart of Rome. The original scheme, best illustrated in a lovely contemporary print, was left uncompleted by Carlisle on the west side while he applied himself to his parkland and temples and obelisks, and finally completed in a correct and duller Palladian manner by another amateur, Sir Thomas Robinson. It hardly seems to matter. Castle Howard is a magic kingdom, best described by Horace Walpole (no admirer of Vanbrugh).

Nobody had infomed me that I should at one view, see a palace, a town, a fortified city, temples on high places, woods worthy of being each a metropolis of the druids, the noblest lawn in the world fenced by half the horizon, and a mausoleum that would tempt one to be buried alive; in short I have seen gigantic palaces before, but never a sublime one.

*The Buildings of England (Yorkshire)

Contemporary with Castle Howard, the two main fronts of Easton Neston in North-
amptonshire are the reworking of a Wren design by his remarkable assistant Nicholas
Hawksmoor, to whom the giant Corinthian order is due.

For those who once thought of Nicholas Hawksmoor as 'the perfect num-ber two' a visit to Easton Neston in Northamptonshire needs to be pre-scribed. Started in the same year as Castle Howard, it is unquestionably Hawksmoor's own design, though (once again) under the benevolent eye of Sir Christopher. Easton Neston, from both its grand and beautiful aspects, while still elaborately classical, has that highly condensed and solemn expression which was later on to be the central characteristic of those almost abstract masterpieces, his London churches. It is a quality which the nimble and pragmatic mind of Wren himself never quite achieved, even for St Paul's Cathedral.

Just as Easton Neston proves that Hawksmoor, as a designer, did not need Vanbrugh, so Vanbrugh's last great house, Seaton Delaval, proves that Vanbrugh did not need Hawksmoor. Over the years, his happy visits to Castle Howard had drawn Vanbrugh powerfully to the north, despite its climate ('There has now fallen a snow up to one's neck . . . in short I am so bloody cold I have almost a mind to Marry and keep myself warm' – which, aged 54, he promptly did, to a Yorkshire squire's daughter aged 25). Creatively, he was at his best there – 'there being many more valuable and agreeable things and places to be seen, than in the tame, sneaking south of England'. Among them, in 1720, was the remote and shabby

Burnt and blackened Seaton Delaval, hard by the North Sea in the Northumberland coalfield, is Vanbrugh's last and most idiosyncratic house, begun in 1718 and completed after he died in 1726.

manor house of old Admiral Delaval, close to the wild Northumberland coast. Do up or tear down? Vanbrugh's advice was of course to demolish and start again.

Seaton Delaval, the house that emerged, was, as usual, extraordinary. One approaches it across an enormous arcaded courtyard with stables and ancillary buildings backed by gloomy woods on either hand. Dead ahead is a square corner-turretted fortress that could have been planned by Smythson, but is elevated by a mind which demonstrates the giant strides that English architecture has taken in a hundred years. The house, monumental but quite small, with only three rooms on the ground floor other than the hall, has all Vanbrugh's mannerisms – round-headed openings, heavily rusticated walls and giant Doric columns, with the widened horizontal joints running straight across them, gloomy recesses, and huge urns dramatising the skyline. But the whole is pure sculpture, and transcends the parts. The Delavals were a wild lot. Fabulous fetes and masquerades astonished the peasantry – tumblings, bull baitings, puppet shows, dancing bears, 'a shift race by women'. Finally, a century later, after the last Delaval had died, the house was consumed by a spectacular fire visible from far out at sea. The blackened and calcined walls that survived have never been rebuilt or even refaced.

Frampton Court near the Severn estuary was designed by a local architect in 1731 under the posthumous influence of Vanbrugh and Hawksmoor. The monumental chimneys are a Vanbrugian feature. OPPOSITE *Chicheley Hall in Buckinghamshire, built around 1700 in the light-hearted Baroque manner popular before the Vanbrugh influence asserted itself.*

The powerful impression made all over England by the work of Vanbrugh and Hawksmoor created the paradox that our architecture became Baroque before it was ever classical: the child preceding the parent. Vanbrugh's inimitable style was unsuccessfully imitated, first at Duncombe Park a few miles from Castle Howard, which has all the weight but none of the wit, and then, for example, at Frampton Court by the Severn in Gloucestershire, which has a truly Vanbrugian density and chunkiness applied to a facade which on a drawing looks quite conventionally Palladian. It was designed by a John Strahan of Bristol, a good copyist described as 'piratical' by Wood of Bath, and has a charming 1750 Gothic villa in its garden. Even merchant's houses in country towns tried to reach for 'massiness', like Fydell House in the centre of Boston, Lincolnshire, and a number in the West Country.

This was an age of great self-confidence (the age of Bach and Handel), which had finally put the traumas of the 17th century behind it. Now architects were emerging everywhere, and not all of them were plagiarists.

Thomas Archer, for example, of a landowning family, who designed the grand four-towered church of St John's, Westminster, had been able to spend four years on the Continent after coming down from Oxford, and unlike Vanbrugh or Hawksmoor had actually studied Borromini's churches in Rome. Chicheley House in Buckinghamshire, confidently attributed to him for stylistic reasons, has an entrance doorcase which can only have come from that source. The way the centre of the house leaps into the air, with the pilasters hoisted up on stilted bases to create the illusion that it thrusts forward, has a stage-set frivolity remote from Vanbrugh's and Hawksmoor's truly three-dimensional compositions.

Archer too found a number of now undocumented imitators. The great red brick house at Hawkstone lies in the flat lands north of Shrewsbury on a wild island of rocky landscape and woodland, topped by a ruined medieval castle complemented by 18th-century follies, now ruined too. The nucleus is a tall pilastered Archeresque house built in 1720 by Sir Richard Hill, then greatly enlarged by his son Sir Rowland around 1750. The low

On an island of rocky and romantic landscape in flat north Shropshire, two generations of the Hill family built the great red and white house of Hawkstone, the central block about 1720, the wings in 1750.

segmental wings end in a pair of taller bow-fronted pavilions, all these curves enhancing the Baroque centrepiece.

But the triumph of English Baroque, celebrated by the completion of Blenheim Palace in 1720, was short-lived. In 1715 the first splendid folio of Colen Campbell's *Vitruvius Britannicus* was published in London. What Inigo Jones had prematurely attempted a century earlier, namely the great *rappel à l'ordre* which would sound the death knell of our architectural 'barbarism', Campbell was now determined to renew and complete. Little is known of the life of this Scot, and it would probably have been nothing at all had his huge book of Palladian designs not attracted the attention of 21-year-old Richard Boyle, the immensely rich Earl of Burlington. To him, this emergence in architecture of a golden age of the arts in England, the fit expression of the country's new found liberty, security and wealth, was a revelation, and soon an obsession. He set off at once on a second visit to Italy to immerse himself in the work of Palladio in Vicenza, and engaged there a young Italian sculptor and an older Yorkshire artist called William Kent, who was studying 'history painting' in Rome. Then immediately on his return he employed Colen Campbell to re-front Burlington House, his great mansion in Piccadilly. But he had taken a much greater liking to Kent, a more relaxed and more stimulating character (a foil to his own austere personality), and for his next and dearest project, the building of a Palladian villa alongside his old manor house at Chiswick (not to live in but to house his collections), it was Kent who did the decor and, in due course, the garden.

The design of the villa itself was entirely Burlington's own. Though we think of it as Palladian, it in fact borrows far less from Palladio's celebrated Villa Rotunda at Vicenza than does Colen Campbell's own design for Mereworth in Kent, which apart from its elevated dome is an almost exact transcription, and appropriately grand in scale and siting. Compared with Mereworth, Chiswick is a toy – 'too little to live in, and too large to hang to one's watch', as Lord Hervey said. This, in fact, is its fascination. Many of its details, like the superbly carved Corinthian portico, the semi-circular windows and the low octagonal dome, as well as the little coffered domes and half domes inside, are taken straight from ancient Rome but miniaturised. The main exceptions are the so-called Venetian windows (you will hardly find any in Venice), of which there are three in a row at the back. This design, with a relieving arch above the familiar three light opening, was taken from Scamozzi, and was to be widely imitated.

OPPOSITE *The Earl of Burlington's little villa at Chiswick west of London was begun in 1725 in the full flood of the Palladian return to the correct classicism Inigo Jones had first introduced a century earlier.* ABOVE *Colen Campbell's design for Mereworth in Kent was a more correct transcription of Palladio's Villa Rotunda at Vicenza, but the elevated dome (through which the flues pass) gives it a very different character.*

This flawless, beautifully carved, Portland Stone 'toy' was the joy of its owner's life. He and Kent continually thought of indoor and outdoor improvements:

> . . . whether it were ordering Indian gauze embroidered with gold and silver flowers for Lady Burlington's dressing table, having a new fringe put on the state bed, varnishing the pictures, redecorating the pantry, having pedestals made for the stone lions and the grand allee, or seeing that the fawns in the park were caught soon after birth and fed with cow's milk.*

Kent was a romantic, temperamentally Baroque, and a secret admirer of Vanbrugh. He was also the most versatile of English artists, least talented in the one art, painting, in which he could be said, after his ten-year stint in Rome, to be a professional. It was he rather than Lancelot (Capability) Brown, who 'leapt the fence, and saw that all Nature was a garden', he, rather than Robert Adam, who first used the spindly grotesque style of neo-Pompeian wall and ceiling decoration, and he, rather than Horace Walpole, who first experimented with Gothic.

---

*James Lees-Milne in *Earls of Creation*.

*The central block at Houghton, designed by Campbell for Sir Robert Walpole in
1721, was originally intended to have pedimented roof pavilions like those at Wilton.
The domes were substituted by the architect James Gibbs.*

But Brown's broad brush, Adam's cool refinement, and Walpole's scholarship were not in his nature, which is most vividly seen in his ponderous gilded furniture, loaded with cherubs, lion's feet, eagle's wings, scallop shells, and blithely heedless of the natural capabilities of wood. It was all imagery, perfectly adapted to the age of the heavy cocked hat, the full-bottomed wig, and the slow creaking state coach, and was only at home in the heavily classical interiors of Wilton, Holkham and Houghton. Of his architecture the two most authentic and characteristic examples are quite modest in scale and date from the early 1740s, at the far end of his career. One is the Worcester Lodge at Badminton, a little classical house riding high on an arched, rusticated base. It contains one splendid room, in his finest Roman manner, in which the Duke of Beaufort would dine with a few friends on summer evenings. The other is a masterpiece – the staircase hall at 44 Berkeley Square – an extraordinary essay in spatial architecture achieved within the width of an ordinary London terrace house: this has to be seen to be believed.

What we above all owe to Kent, and to Alexander Pope who inspired him, is that the great Palladian houses are not set in equally formal geometrical gardens as they would have been in France, but in 'Elysian fields', evocations of the romantic groves and waterfalls and temples of Italy.

William Kent's little lodge at Badminton has an elevated and elegant dining room where the Duke of Beaufort could entertain a few friends by candlelight.

Stourhead in Wiltshire is a Campbell design of 1720, but the wings were not added until the end of the century and the portico, all to the original design, in 1841. OPPOSITE *Campbell's little garden pavilion, grandly known as Ebberstone Hall, can be seen from the main road to Scarborough. Behind it there was a garden of cascades, now vanished.*

Stourhead in Wiltshire is a famous case in point. This Arcadian garden, with its artificial lake and romantically sited temples, is the perfect complement to Colen Campbell's austere, beautifully proportioned, east-facing house – a rare example of the architect's intentions faithfully carried out over more than a century (central block 1722, wings 1796, portico 1840) – and then well restored after a fire in 1902. It therefore gives an impression of complete authenticity, and of that restful predominence of wall over window which is the hallmark of the Palladian house, when one compares it with late 17th-century houses like Uppark and Chicheley. Best visited on winter days, when one can read the whole frontage through the trees in

pure elevation, as in Campbell's original engravings, these houses have no texture – none of the 'tactile values' by which Bernard Berenson, writing in the 1930s, assessed Renaissance art. In the words of another scholar, Rudolf Wittkower, 'Italian architecture must always be judged by its plastic values; an English 18th-century building should be seen from a distance, like a picture'.

This is equally true of Campbell's much grander house of the same date, Houghton, though the Yorkshire stone of which it is built does not have the brilliant sharpness of Portland, and the picture here is distorted by the four squat corner domes rather naughtily added by James Gibbs, a

mannerist of the school of Wren, best known for St Martin's in the Fields in London and the Radcliffe Camera in Oxford. Campbell's original design, with corner pavilions as at Wilton, is much more clearly in the Jonesian tradition. Sir Robert Walpole, for whom it was designed, is the prototype of the *nouveau riche*, not to say complacent, Whig grandees who dominated the arts of the early Georgian age. For such men, with their Roman and Renaissance collections, their beautiful, leather-bound libraries, their great hierarchy of servants, and their highly formal entertaining, Kent's grandiose interiors and furniture are exactly right. The great cube-shaped Stone Hall and the sumptuous Saloon, completed by 1732, are plainly an elaboration of the style introduced by Inigo Jones a century earlier.

Despite his immense wealth, the cost of Houghton broke even Walpole, and he died heavily in debt: his entire collection of pictures had to be sold in 1779 to the Empress Catherine of Russia.

Just as Catherine, like Peter the Great before her, was obsessed with the Westernisation of their semi-barbarous empire, so the Georgian aristocracy were determined to demonstrate the cultural affinities of their remote island with Italy and the prestige of its military victories over France. While Continental architecture moved from the flamboyant to the frivolous, therefore, English country houses and fashionable town architecture remained solidly Roman, its statesmen were memorialised in toga and sandals, its poetry was Augustan, and its gardens and landscape were transformed into damper versions of the Campagna. Up in Yorkshire, for example, whether it was a tiny bungalow on the main road to Scarborough or the huge Lascelles mansion at Harewood, Campbell and his followers had only to reach for the Vitruvian rule book and Leoni's version of Palladio's *Quattro Libri*, of which the first translation appeared in the same year (1715) as the first volume of his own *Vitruvius Britannicus*.

These were, of course, up-market, expensive books, but they were soon complemented by manuals of all kinds, often produced under the patronage of the great Whig landowners, some for the use of minor country gentry, some for craftsmen, some for gardeners. It was this flood of literature, more than the example of the Great, that produced the decent, middle-sized Georgian box that appeared in every country town and village, often a simple recasing of a 16th- or 17th-century manor house.

Even the most exalted of the Palladian grandees were not above acting as architects, presumably without charge. The Earl of Burlington (to some raised eyebrows) designed a ballroom for the burghers of York and a dormitory for Westminster School; the Earl of Pembroke designed White Lodge in Richmond Park for George II, with the help of his favourite architect, Roger Morris, in the coolest Burlington manner. Sir Thomas Robinson, the rich and extravagant Yorkshire landowner, rebuilt his own house, Rokeby, also in the Burlington manner as early as 1725, and later added a wing to Castle Howard for Lord Carlisle, his father-in-law, and designed Claydon House for Lord Verney.

Unlike Sir Thomas, Sir Francis Dashwood was no architect, but rather one of the many amateurs who, on the strength of a Grand Tour, by picking the brains of his friends, and with some technical help from a local man, was able to rebuild his own house in high Palladian style in the middle half of the century. West Wycombe is a collection of elevations, each very fine in itself, but none having any relationship with its neighbours, in a way that no architect, trained to think three-dimensionally, would have contemplated. It was hoped, but never quite achieved, to conceal the corners by planting. The north front, commanding the ideal 18th-century landscape, was the first built, and is correctly Palladian, with arched windows in the centrepiece not at all spoilt, for once, by their Victorian glazing. The east is a Doric portico, a replica of the four at Mereworth, the home of Dashwood's uncle. The south range is a transcription, unique in England, of Palladio's Palazzo Chiericati at Vicenza, lovely to look at, but not much fun for the children and servants tucked in under the upper colonnade. Finally the entrance portico on the

West Wycombe in Buckinghamshire was built after 1750 by the amateur of architecture Sir Francis Dashwood. It is an essay in classical plagiarism. The east portico (OPPOSITE) is a replica of Mereworth. The later west portico (ABOVE) is by the Grecian scholar Nicholas Revett, and the wide south side with its double tier of loggias (LEFT) is inspired by a Palladio palace in Vicenza.

99

PRECEDING PAGES *Provinvial Palladian: Dalemain on the shores of Ullswater in the English Lakes.* ABOVE *The restrained and elegant front of Dalemain is nine bays long, and built in a local pinkish-grey limestone. The family for which it was built still live in it.*

west, the last to be built, reflects Dashwood's conversion to the Grecian taste, and is a copy by Nicholas Revett of the Temple of Bacchus in Telos, Ionia. The house's lovely interior has been splendidly restored by the present Sir Francis.

On a smaller scale, I take two much less grand Palladian houses, at opposite ends of England, to represent this great mass of Gentlemen's Architecture. One is Dalemain, close to Ullswater in the Lake District, built of the local pinkish limestone by a family which still lives in it – a perfectly proportioned classic design of the 1740s, nine windows long, with the five central ones given emphasis by corner quoins and an appro-

priately simple doorcase. The other, Came House near Dorchester, Dorset, is about the same size, but more dressy, if now more weather-worn. It was built in 1754 for the Damer family by Francis Cartwright, one of the cheerful group of provincial architects who rebuilt Blandford after it was destroyed by fire, and its perfectly proportioned north front overlooks the quietly pastoral valley of the Came. Close by, on the Dorchester road, is a graceful, symmetrical pink house of the same period which must be one of the few thatched rectories in England (see page 5).

Compared with the proliferation of amateur architecture in the reign of the first two Georges, the output of the professional Palladians, the

*Provincial Palladian in Dorset: Came House in its quiet pastoral valley was designed
in the 1750s by a local architect of Blandford in a surprisingly grand manner.*

architects of the School of Burlington, was obviously less extensive and on the whole less interesting. The leading lights, with large London practices, were James Paine and Sir Roger Taylor, both of whom remained staunch Palladians through careers which lasted until the 1780s. Paine's grandest country house is Kedleston, of which the splendid winged plan (clearly intended to outdo Kent's palace for Lord Leicester at Holkham) was only half built, but nevertheless can be appreciated in all its spacious glory from across the lake to the north. Heveningham in Suffolk, Taylor's great house for the Vanneck family, is comparatively two-dimensional, with only one effective viewpoint, also across water

to the north. This is the encasing in a grandiose Corinthian order, with appropriate wings, of a simple brick box of the 17th century. The house, alas recently severely damaged by fire, contains what has seemed to me to be the most beautiful room in England – the vaulted Hall designed by James Wyatt.

More interesting than either of these two successful Londoners are two provincials of a rather later generation. The first is John Carr (1723-1807), the son of a Yorkshire mason and quarry owner. Having made his name among the local gentry for his design for a new grandstand for York Races, Carr went on to set up the first major provincial practice in the United

Constable Burton lies in the wide pastures of lower Wensleydale, an impeccable design of the 1760s by John Carr of York, with a recessed portico approached by a wide Palladian staircase. OPPOSITE *Heveningham in Suffolk, recently badly damaged by fire, has a fan-vaulted hall by James Wyatt in the Adam manner, even more exquisite than Robert Adam's own version at Kenwood.*

Kingdom. All his work was of superb quality, and two of his houses, one in the north and one in the south, could not have been bettered by Burlington himself. Constable Burton in the dales near Leyburn (1762) is a simple and impeccable transcription of Scamozzi's villa Rocca Pisani (1576), with acknowledgements, of course, to Chiswick as well. Basildon, in Capability Brown parkland looking northwards across the Thames to the wooded ridges and combes of the Chilterns, is another copybook example, close in date to Campbell's Stourhead, and equally impeccably proportioned.

These two contrast interestingly in their entrance arrangements. The Italian *piano nobile*, at the head of a formal staircase, adopted undeviatingly by all the Palladians, consigned the ground level to a supportive role succinctly described by Lord Hervey (in regard to Houghton) as useful for 'hunters, hospitality, noise, dirt, and business'. To reach the State Rooms above you could go up indoors via a grand staircase magnificently handled by Kent at Holkham, by Paine at Wardour, and ingeniously, within the portico, by Carr at Basildon. But this consigned the front door to insignificance. Externally, the divided staircase, first displayed in full grandeur by Burlington himself at Chiswick and later by Carr at Constable Burton, stages a far more splendid arrival (though of course a damp one in bad weather).

For the Royal Crescent in Bath (1765) John Wood the younger adopts the Jonesian model, applies it to a great flattened horseshoe plan, and sets it in open landscape.

This was just one example of the Palladian sacrifice of convenience to effect. Alexander Pope, as usual, brilliantly satirises the whole movement in his Epistle to Lord Burlington.

You show us Rome was glorious, not profuse,
And pompous buildings once were things of Use.
Yet shall (my Lord) your just, your noble rules,
Fill half the land with Imitating Foolls;
Who random drawings from your sheets shall take,
And of one beauty many blunders make;
Load some vain Church with old Theatric state,
Turn Arcs of Triumph to a Garden-gate;
Reverse your Ornaments; and hang them all
On some patch'd dog-hole ek'd with ends of wall;
Then clap four slices of Pilaster on't,
That, lac'd with bits of rustic, makes a Front;
Shall call the winds thro' long arcades to roar,
Proud to catch cold at a Venetian door;
Conscious they act a true Palladian part,
And if they starve, they starve by rules of art.

The other highly distinguished provincial firm was that of the John Woods (father and son) in Bath; and their work brings us back to the story of the town-house in England. The contrast with the Continent is again most striking. 'Banishment alone', wrote Arthur Young, 'will force the French to execute what the English do from pleasure – reside upon and adorn their estates.' Few were the noble families who could afford or could be bothered to build a London house large enough for balls and assemblies, and none of those mansions that survive are comparable in scale or beauty with the Parisian hotels of the Marais and St Germain. Most were consequently abandoned by their owners to commercial interests in the 1930s. Only Spencer House, recently superbly renovated, still presents a splendid Palladian front to Green Park. For those who once owned land on the western fringes of the city, it was much more fun (and might recoup some of their overspending in the provinces) to go into speculative building for the benefit of the 'middling sort' of Londoners – the new bourgeoisie who could in turn recoup by renting out their houses to country families for the summer Season. The London landowners themselves seldom

A rare survivor of the style in which London was rebuilt after the Great Fire, these houses in Clapham have the wooden cornice and sash-windows flush with the wall which fire regulations later made illegal in the capital. OPPOSITE *The Circus in Bath built by John Wood the elder just before he died. Consciously adapted from the super-imposed Orders of the Colosseum in Rome, the Circus closes the vistas from three converging streets.*

built, preferring to sell building leases to developers with a far sounder and surer architectural touch than their successors of later centuries.

So it was that the London terrace house, first tried out (as we have seen) in Covent Garden and Lincoln's Inn, came into its own. John Summerson has quoted a French visitor: 'These narrow houses, three or four storeys high – one for eating, one for sleeping, a third for company, a fourth underground for the kitchen, a fifth perhaps at top for the servants – and the agility, the ease, the quickness with which the individuals of the family run up and down, and perch on the different storeys, give the idea of a cage with its sticks and birds.'

Inigo Jones had based his Lincoln's Inn Fields' elevations on the classical principle of the ground floor as Base, the first and second for the pilasters of the Order, and an Attic, tucked away behind the parapet above the cornice. But it was a century before the Palladians returned to this simple and satisfactory device. The rebuilding after the Great Fire took the form we can still see in some of London's villages (Clapham for example), with wooden cornices and tiled roofs, or in a more sophisticated form in Queen Anne's Gate, with its very special carved pine doorheads – or indeed in the main streets of red brick Georgian towns like Pershore and Farnham. It was not until the London Building Acts of the early 1700s that, for fire

protection, the wood cornice was banned and the sash windows were required to sit back four and a half inches, a half brick, behind the wall face, and these rules controlled the great upsurge of speculative building that followed the Peace of Utrecht in 1713.

The first two speculatively built squares in London, soon after the Restoration, were Bloomsbury and St James's, originally designed by their promoters, Lords Southampton and St Albans, as settings for their own mansions. There ensued the destruction in 1666 of the City by fire, and the resulting building boom was inevitably concentrated on its devastated core and sites immediately west of it. None of those wood-corniced and casemented houses has survived, and, when peace brought the next boom in 1714, developers moved further west along the Oxford Street axis. A group of Whig gentlemen laid out Hanover Square and built St George's Church in the 1720s, followed by the Grosvenor Estate, centred on Grosvenor Square, and the Cavendish/Harley Estate, a Tory enterprise centred on Cavendish Square. But such attempts as there were to achieve symmetry and Palladian order in the new squares came to nothing: each turned out a miscellany of brown or red brick Georgian houses, and no attempt was made to coordinate the joints between the different estates.

For this achievement we have to turn to the Woods of Bath. John Wood the elder, like Carr, was a Yorkshireman, but came to London as an apprentice builder/architect and almost certainly took lodgings in Oxford Street, in the heart of the West End developments. He seems to have worked closely with Edward Sheppard, who attempted a pedimented Palladian group in Grosvenor Square and designed the Duke of Chandos's elegant pair of Palladian houses in Cavendish Square. Bath had recently come into fashion through the energy of Beau Brummel, and John Wood had brought with him from Yorkshire some ideas for four areas ripe for development, in which he was able to interest an early-bird developer, Robert Gay. In 1727, to start the ball rolling, Wood moved to Bath with a team of craftsmen, and embarked on a speculation of his own, Queen's

Square. Here he was able to achieve the symmetrical stone terrace-as-palace concept which had never yet materialised in London, the elevation of course faithfully Jonesian.

Wood knew Bath had been a Roman city and was determined, on the little he had read about the Imperial City, to take this as his theme, but it was not until the 1750s that he was able to pull it off. The Circus is an extraordinary combination of the *rond point* where rides meet in the forests of France, entered in this case by three evenly spaced streets, and the superimposed Orders of the Colosseum – in a miniature version described by Smollet as 'a pretty bauble and looks like Vespasian's amphitheatre turned inside out'. The little Circus now is regrettably dwarfed by enormous trees and would be finer without them.

The *rond-point* idea liberated English town planning from its boring London rectangularity, and was immediately exploited by John Wood the younger to lead out west to the great slope on which he built his Royal Crescent, another concept with a glorious future. This is no bauble, but a grandiose Ionic parade on a scale no group of houses had ever aspired to. Bath had taken off, as had the Jonesian elevation – Base, Order (applied or implied), and Attic – which was to dominate British town design well into the 19th century. In Bath itself crescents displayed themselves joyfully across the wooded sun-soaked slopes, the most remarkable the serpentine Lansdown Crescent, rather fancifully seen by Siegfried Giedion, a modernist writer of the 1930s, as derived from Borromini's undulating walls and inspiring Le Corbusier's wavy model for the rebuilding of Algiers.

Following the Bath example, all three of the British capitals and their successors overseas adopted the Square, the Circus and the Crescent as their components, and so did the seaside resorts and spas that proliferated over the next hundred years. Carr of York built one of the finest crescents for the Duke of Devonshire at Buxton, taking as his model, once again, Inigo Jones and his Piazzas at Covent Garden.

CHAPTER 5

The Augustan Age

Fitzroy Square in London.

IN THE END, AS IS INEVITABLE, THE MODEL STARTED TO PALL. Pope had seen this coming and so had Horace Walpole, in natural reaction to his father's taste. But the changes that occurred in England in the early years of George III were much more profound than mere changes in taste. The population of England, at six million, was only half that of France, but it was a much more mobile and ingenious population, intensely patriotic, and united in sentiment since the Jacobites had finally been seen off and the French defeated in India. There would be no more copying of foreign fashions. Shocking though its extremes of wealth and poverty may seem to us, they were moderate by Continental standards and mitigated by many charities. Innovation, whether in farming methods, road and canal building or in industrial machinery, could spread downwards from aristocratic experiment or upwards from craftsmen's in-genuity, and was continually refreshed by the flood of wealth from the American colonies and the Caribbean. With the increasing skill of the foundries and the landing of new hardwoods, all artifacts from frigates to phaetons and from chairs to shotguns had become more spare, elegant and functional. Architecture must, as always, reflect the new age, the age in which the dashing Mr and Mrs Coltman, in Joseph Wright of Derby's marvellous picture in the National Gallery, were representative of the younger generation. To such people, the grandiose Palladian interior seemed pompous and pretentious.

The man who set himself to meet their desires – to outdate Palladian just as Burlington had outdated the Baroque – was Robert Adam. And it was typical of the new age that the innovators should be not Whig aris-tocrats but professional architects. The Adam brothers, whose father

PRECEDING PAGES *The north front of Kedleston, as built to Paine's original design.*
OPPOSITE *The saloon below the dome at Kedleston is in Robert Adam's most solemn
Roman manner.*

Matthew Brettingham's plan for Kedleston, with four pavilions linked by quadrant colonnades, was retained by Paine for the north front and by Adam for the south, from which one enters the Saloon (A) and the marble Hall (B).

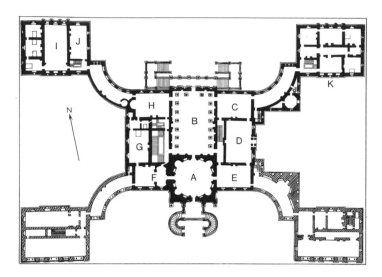

OPPOSITE *The marble Hall seen from the main entrance, looking towards the Saloon. The Corinthian colonnade is of pink Nottinghamshire alabaster.*

William had been a dullish Burlingtonian architect in Edinburgh, were a tight-knit family firm, as well balanced and as conscious of their public image as any commercial company of the 1990s. The oldest, John, was the financial backer, the second, Robert, the creative artist, the third, James, the scholar and the fourth, William Junior, the loyal but not very capable business manager. And in contrast to the rigidity of Burlington and his admirers, the Adams were a far more flexible and more pragmatic outfit, both in their philosophy and in their practice.

This was no revolution. Robert Adam never dreamed of throwing the classical Orders overboard, but proposed to apply them with more finesse and with a deeper understanding of history. But to reach this he had to pick his way through a controversy that was at its height when he arrived in Rome in 1756. This was due to the discoveries of the architecture of Ancient Greece, initiated by scholars like Le Roy and Winckelmann. Under the patronage of the Society of Dilettanti (of which Sir Francis Dashwood had been a founder member) English architect/archaeologists like Robert Wood, James Stewart and Nicholas Revett had brought the message to England – the message that Vitruvius was not the once-and-for-all authority, that the Romans were really copyists, that the fountain-head of European architecture was Greece. This was violently contested by the Romans, and in particular by the dramatic drawings and passionate propaganda of Piranesi.

Robert and James Adam, the coolest of Scots, typical of their generation in their dislike of Enthusiasm, refused to take sides. Neither Greek temples nor Palladio's formulations had the light touch they were looking for. This they found by taking a side-step into the rather mannered classicism of the third-century Emperor Diocletian's enormous palace at Spalato (far more appropriate than the sixth century BC), in the newly unearthed murals at Pompeii and in the 'grotesque' or 'arabesque' decor of Raphael's loggia in the Vatican and in the Villa Madama. From these sources (the last already plundered by others) they put together a style, a fashion, a manner

that was irresistible; but it was not a new architecture or an expression of genius at the level of Vanbrugh, as Robert always generously recognised.

In fact he never had the same opportunities – never once built a great house from scratch. The second age of the great country palaces, inaugurated by Castle Howard, was drawing to an end, and was soon to be deferred for half a century by the American and the Napoleonic wars. Robert Adam's country house work consisted entirely in the completion, alteration, or decoration of buildings begun by others. Of these one of the first, and in the end perhaps the most important, is Kedleston. Lord Scarsdale was rich enough, and rough enough, to dismiss Paine and commission the newly fashionable Adam to redesign the two (out of four) unbuilt wings and the south front. Alas, the wings remained unbuilt, but the south front is a graceful combination of the temple of Jupiter at Spalato (illustrated in Adam's book on the Palace) and the contemporary Arch of Constantine in Rome. A recent writer* charmingly describes the relationship of 'the crab pincer staircase and the shallow dome, which looks as if it might have floated up from the embrace of those curving arms to settle discreetly behind the triumphal arch'. The great rooms beyond it, the pillared hall with its magnificent range of scagliola columns and the round saloon below the dome, are unsurpassed by any in England, even by the same architect at Syon, the Duke of Northumberland's great house near London. Sir John Soane, a not uncritical admirer, who bought all Adam's drawings for his Museum, was so taken by the frontispiece at Kedleston that he could not resist borrowing the idea for his own house in Middlesex, transposing it into his preferred, more Grecian, Ionic order.

The Adams, like the Woods, were tempted to invest in real estate, but on a considerably greater scale, and unlike the Woods they made a hash of it. Their Adelphi terraces fronting the Thames near Charing Cross in

---

*Olive Cook in *The English Country House* (1974).

*Robert Adam's remarkable south front also derives from classical Rome – a transcrip-
tion of the Arch of Constantine on the Forum. The idea was later borrowed (but with
Greek detail) by Sir John Soane for his country house.* OPPOSITE *The east side of
Fitzroy Square is a late and sophisticated design by Robert Adam, and is rare among
London squares in being faced in Portland stone.*

London were a financial disaster, hurting their reputation and their
friends' pockets despite the skills in self promotion attested by their three-
volume *Works in Architecture of Robert and James Adam*. Nor was the rather
finicky result substantial enough for its prominent site, suffering by com-
parison with Somerset House, down-river masterpiece of their arch-rival,
the distinguished official architect, Sir William Chambers.

As an urban architect Robert Adam did finally redeem himself, late in
life, in Fitzroy Square, one of the very few London squares to be built in
superb Portland stone. The east block is a complex and sculptural classical
design, exhibiting what Adam had many years earlier described as 'move-

ment', a Baroque quality mastered by Vanbrugh and well examplified in
the Horse Guards building by William Kent – a designer for whom Adam
had no use at all.

Among the many ironies of the Adam phenomenon is that some of the
best Adamesque buildings were done by their imitators. In Mountsorrel, a
small town in the Midlands, is a group of houses by an unknown architect
which gracefully evoke his style, and in all Britain there are no finer
'Adam' houses than those of James Wyatt, the dissolute and disorganised
young designer of Castle Coole in County Fermanagh and of Heaton Hall
in Manchester – the latter also, on its comparatively modest scale, a more

OPPOSITE *The delicate and graceful style Adam later adopted for his interiors appears in this house in the Leicestershire village of Mountsorrel, the work of an unknown designer.* ABOVE *James Wyatt's Heaton Hall near Manchester (1770) is in his best Adam manner, and gracefully composed about a central rotunda using an Ionic order with 'Venetian' windows.*

mature demonstration of movement than anything Robert was able to build. Heaton is also one of the first classical houses to drop off its rusticated base on to the ground, and thereby further exemplify the retreat from Palladian grandeur.

But while some of the best 'Adam' work was done by his successors, so was a great deal of the worst. Well on into the 20th century every doctor's waiting room in Harley Street was finished off with an 'Adam' ceiling straight out of the plasterer's catalogue. Soane, as usual, gives a final judgement: 'Mr Adam also deserves great praise for banishing from interior decorations the heavy architectural ornaments, which prevailed in all our

buildings before his time; although it will be admitted that he sometimes indulged in the extreme of fancy and lightness.'

If James Wyatt was the most talented though most uncouth of the Adam generation, Henry Holland was the most tasteful and most reliable. Like Wyatt, Holland was one of a family of builders and architects, born and practising almost exclusively in London, and his entree into the country house world was ensured by his becoming the junior partner, and in due course the son-in-law, of Capability Brown. So while his *magnum opus*, the Prince Regent's Carlton House, was to vanish without trace before long, as did his neat 'pavilion' at the north end of Cadogan Square,

Berrington Hall in Herefordshire is an early work (1778) of Henry Holland, later the Prince Regent's architect. With its plain round-headed windows and simple doorway, the house has no Palladian pretensions to grandeur. OPPOSITE *Holland's interiors at Berrington profited from the increased prosperity of the Harley family. The staircase lands under a glass dome, with recesses screened by scagliola columns.*

there survives from quite early in his career the most perfect of his country houses, Berrington in Herefordshire.

It was built around 1780 for Thomas Harley, a younger son of the Earl of Oxford, who had done well in the City and became Lord Mayor, and later a popular Member of Parliament for Hereford. The house is built to a severely neo-Classic design in the local warm pink sandstone, and stands high in a spacious park, its portico facing west into the wild hills of Wales. The central pair of unfluted Ionic columns are widely spaced in a welcoming gesture, and beyond them is a tall, slim, round-headed door, quite plain except for a pair of typically chaste draped plaques on either hand.

The house is however usually entered from the symmetrical courtyard at the back, through a doorway unfortunately moved off-centre in a rather confused and poky 19th-century rearrangement. Arched openings are repeated around the upper storey of the house and the lower story of the wings.

Harley had no sons, but his daughter Anne married the eldest son of the celebrated Admiral Lord Rodney, who would inherit the house. The interior is consequently more elaborate than was originally intended, with naval references in the Adamesque plasterwork and chimney pieces, and a dramatic staircase leading up to a domed upper hall with elegant

Bedford Square (1775), symmetrical on all four sides, shows how the Woods' ideal of the terrace as palace was simplified for London. It is almost style-less, with stucco replacing stone for the central features and door arches.

Corinthian columns. The pretty glazed dome and the fine staircase balustrade are built of cast iron from Coalbrookdale.

Holland's remodelling of Southill in Bedfordshire, done 15 years later, is far more restrained (partly no doubt in deference to Samuel Whitbread's more austere taste), and illustrates the stripped-down, almost styleless late Georgian front that was now the staple ingredient of London's expanding West End. Its only ornaments are the verandahs, a return to the Elizabethan loggia with its purely decorative use of the Orders. These paired Ionic arcades were soon to become a favourite device of John Nash, as in the twin quadrants of Park Crescent in London. And Southill, too, like Heaton and Wyatt's Doddington in Gloucestershire, sits right down on the ground.

The styleless, or astylar, London terrace house, graded like men of war into four classes from first rate to fourth, started life in Bloomsbury, where it survives in what the Victorians thought deeply depressing numbers. One sees it at its best in Bedford Square, begun in 1775, where for the first time in London the example of Queen's Square in Bath is followed, with each side of the square handled as a single palace, but with none of John Wood's Palladian pretensions. Cornices are plain, windows without architraves, front doors have no classical surrounds except moulded voussoirs in the newly patented Coade Stone composition. Only the centrepieces of each block have Adamesque pediments and pilasters in the stucco, another cheap imitation of stone, which before long was to take over vast tracts of the northern and western extensions of London.

It must have seemed in the 1760s, as it did two centuries later, that we had all the answers. A people confident of its own genius, the British had found a formula for the design and layout of town houses which had been honed to perfection over a hundred years. In the landscape Capability Brown, shedding Kent's Italianate ornaments, had developed a theory based on the simple rule: 'Consult the Genius of the Place in all.' Regular, classical architecture set in irregular romantic landscape must have seemed an immutable principle. But then, in the second half of the century, it all began to fall apart, not because of slumps, wars, or revolutions, but because of a new factor (or new since the fall of Rome) – boredom.

CHAPTER 6

The Picturesque

Most dramatic of all the Regency fantasies was Wyatt's Fonthill Abbey.

T HE ROMANTIC MOVEMENT, AS IT CAME TO BE CALLED, MAY have culminated in the French Revolution, in the glories and disasters of Napoleon, but it began in frivolity and even silliness – girls swooning over Gothic novels, tramps paid to squat all summer in artificial hermitages, the Welsh mountains written up as 'our British Alps'. For architecture the most significant movement of the mid-century was the rediscovery, half serious, half for fun, of the Middle Ages. It was serious as a reassertion of mystery, sentiment and chivalry in a materialist and rationalist society; it was for fun in the rediscovery of Gothic (in the first place by classical architects like Kent and Chambers) as a decorative language for minor buildings. Horace Walpole's Strawberry Hill, its most dramatic example, was a demonstration both of genuine scholarship and of enjoyable protest against the conventional taste of

Adam England. But it was a facelift applied to an old building: it was not architecture.

Downton Castle on the borders of Hereford and Shropshire is a milestone for the development of the English house; it was begun 20 years before Henry Holland's chaste Southill. The word picturesque did not exist until the 18th century, when it came into use, naturally, for landscapes, whether wild or man-made. Its application, in theory, to buildings was the work of two neighbouring landowners on the Welsh borders – Sir Uvedale Price and Richard Payne Knight, who defined it (in terms deeply shocking to Palladians) as 'the blending and melting together of objects together with a playful and airy lightness and a sort of loose indistinction'. Less obscurely, one can say that the essence was that buildings should not dominate landscapes but become equal partners in creating the kind of

PRECEDING PAGES *Belsay Hall in Northumberland, begun in 1810, was the result of an enthusiast's visit to Athens. One enters the great square, smooth, stone house, raised on a stepped podium like a Greek temple, under enormous Doric columns supporting a correct frieze and cornice.* OPPOSITE *The Regency fashion for exotic styles is demonstrated at Sezincote in Gloucestershire, designed by Samuel Pepys Cockerell for his brother Sir Charles, who was an Indian nabob.*

*Downton in Herefordshire was the prototype for another Picturesque fashion, the
fake castle. It was designed as early as 1772 by a local squire, Richard Payne Knight.
Its interiors are conventionally Georgian.*

picture their owners enjoyed – that is to say, the romantic landscapes of
painters like Salvator Rosa and Claude Lorraine. Knight's 'castle' is not
Gothic, but it is obviously, flamboyantly picturesque – 'a picture', in fact,
as people say to this day. That the interior is conventionally classical is a
contradiction which did not bother him at all.

Once you had made your escape from ancient Rome, you could build in
any style that amused you. Sir William Chambers, who had travelled ex-
tensively, made even Chinese respectable by erecting a pagoda at Kew; Stewart
and Revett introduced Periclean Athenian, which after a slow start was to be
all the rage during the Regency; and before long a retired nabob of the East

India Company was to build himself a large country house at Sezincote in
Gloucestershire in a remarkably correct version of the architecture of the
Moguls. To achieve this Sir Charles Cockerell, the owner (whose brother
was the architect), took the advice of the celebrated topographical artist of
India, Thomas Daniell, and also of Humphrey Repton, then engaged on
sketches for the Brighton Pavilion, who persuaded the Prince Regent to go
down to see the house. But all these styles, like 18th-century Gothic,
started life under the free and easy regime of the Picturesque – a sideline
for serious architects – and no one could have predicted that two of them,
the Grecian and the Gothic, would grow up to be taken seriously.

*Sezincote's Mogul architecture had few imitators, but the house was visited when
barely finished by the Prince Regent to get ideas for his Brighton Pavilion.*

Meanwhile, the amateur country-gentleman architects had a final fling before the professionals took over. The best of them was undoubtedly Sir Roger Newdigate of Arbury in Warwickshire, the founder of the famous poetry prize at Oxford. Like Strawberry Hill, which it closely followed, his house is a recasing and extension of an older one, but its exterior is symmetrically composed and its interior is a marvel of filigree Gothic elegance, outdoing Walpole at his own game.

Arbury is tucked away among lakes in a Midland valley, not far from Coventry. Leighton Hall in wild North Lancashire, although later in date, is a much less sophisticated design, but this is its charm, and its situation

is breathtaking. To the south a vast, sheep-cropped, oak-studded park rises gently upwards, while to the north the pale limestone house has as backcloth the dark, mysterious forest of Furness. As architecture, Leighton is nothing much: it is scenery, it is the epitome of the Picturesque.

One of the most endearing efforts of the amateurs is Nether Winchendon House, in a remote timber hamlet in the Vale of Aylesbury. Inherited in 1780 by Scrope Bernard, younger son of a governor of New Jersey and Massachussets, this timber-framed Tudor mansion was extended in brick and stone, tied together by Gothic cresting, given wood-framed Gothic windows and a bold arched entrance screen, the whole coming together

The fan vaulting of the Saloon at Arbury, and the Alhambra-like plasterwork of its bow window, were designed by Henry Keene. OPPOSITE *Sir Roger Newdigate started Gothicising his old house, Arbury Hall, near Coventry, as early as 1748, the same year as Horace Walpole started doing the same at Strawberry Hill.* NEXT PAGES *Leighton Hall in north Lancashire is a modest Georgian house charmingly Gothicised using a very pale stone in the 19th century.*

more by luck than design – then abandoned by its owner because his wife had never liked it. (However, the family still lives there.)

But the most extravagant and eccentric of them all was William Beckford of Fonthill, the fabulously rich West Indian merchant who in 1796 persuaded James Wyatt to build him a towering Gothic 'abbey' among his remote Wiltshire woodlands. The four slim arms of this cross-shaped building met in a tall octagon with a great tower superimposed upon it – a folly exceeded in scale only by the fairy castles of the mad Ludwig II of Bavaria. Its collapse in 1825 deprived the infant Gothic Revival of its most spectacular monument.

All this *fin-de-siècle* escapism, this cult of the amazing, was something new in architectural history. What lay behind it? The fact was that the ground which had seemed so solid under the feet of the Adam generation was beginning to shake. Most of the largest buildings of the late Georgian era were not houses at all. They were mills. And soon, in the pretty steel engravings of the early 19th century, behind the bosky romantic landscape, there would be a tell-tale plume of smoke, and among the forests of masts of our expanding fleets would be a pinnace or two with a black stovepipe funnel. If you belonged to a family with a coat of arms or aspired to become one, you wished all the more for your refaced or brand-new home

OPPOSITE *Nether Winchendon House in the Vale of Aylesbury is a basically medie-*
val house, first Tudorised, then Georgianised, then — about 1780 — re-Gothicised
and battlemented. ABOVE *One approaches Nether Winchendon through this Geor-*
gian Gothic arcade, through which the windows of the Hall can be seen on the far
side of the gravelled courtyard.

to reflect its genuine or bogus antiquity in its architecture. As now, such
people preferred "the olden time" to their own.

The subterranean rumblings were not only those of machinery. There
was the roar of Revolution. The fear of Jacobinism haunted the night
thoughts of the old landed gentry and the new rich. It was no time to be
building enormous mansions. For the first time since the Middle Ages, and
for the first 30 years of the new century, it would be public rather than
domestic architecture which would make the running.

Both the two great figures of the new age, Nash and Soane, exemplified
this change. John Nash (1752-1815) was a Londoner, a convivial, optimistic

man entirely without the indolence that had handicapped Wyatt. Trained
in the office of the conservative Sir Robert Taylor, bankrupted
at the age of 25 by failing to sell two conventionally Palladian houses
in Bloomsbury Square, he fled the city for a decade and seemed to
have wholly missed out on the Adam boom. Instead, living and working in Wales, he was captivated by the Uvedale Price/Payne Knight circle
and their notion of architecture as scenery, and with it a broad-
brush, slapdash attitude to detail that characterised his whole output
and shocked knowledgeable critics. He also had the wit to see that
grand houses were out and that toy castles, villas, and even thatched

Helmingham in Suffolk is another, much grander, hybrid, with a wide moat, draw-
bridge and Tudor gateway, surrounded by good Regency Gothic done by John Nash
in the 1800s and remodelled in 1841. OPPOSITE *Nash's several castles include this*
little one in south Devon, Luscombe, almost lost in the wide park and woodlands
landscaped for the Hoare family by his partner Humphrey Repton.

cottages were in. What fun it all was! For some years he formed a partnership with his contemporary, Humphrey Repton, who had succeeded
Lancelot Brown as the fashionable landscapist of the age. Repton's attitude
to landscape, less stereotyped than Brown's and less extravagant (he liked
to claim 'a just sense of general utility') suited the modest size of
Nash's houses and their client's pockets. Luscombe Castle in Devon is a
perfect example of their collaboration, and in its modest size it is an
example of the change of scale in that it was commissioned by the
nephew of the rich banker for whom Colen Campbell had designed
grandiose Stourhead.

For his castles, and more significantly for his villas, Nash was able to
make a complete escape from symmetry (not easy for a classically trained
architect) in a natural and relaxed way which the Victorians often
found difficult, and would never have credited to him because of their
moral disapproval of his work. This was mainly due to his predilection for
stucco, a material which they regarded as a cheap, nasty, and dishonest
substitute for stone. Cronkhill in Shropshire, a pretty Italianate villa
built by Lord Berwick of Attingham for his agent, is a charming
example both of the compact informality and of the stucco. It was the
harbinger of the assortment of stucco villas in various mildly incorrect

OPPOSITE *Another favourite Regency subject was the* cottage ornée. *This one is in the pretty Berkshire village of Sulham, close to the Thames.* RIGHT *This stucco villa, Cronkhill near Shrewsbury, was built by Nash in 1802 for the agent to the Attingham estate. With its round tower and loggia, it was the first free-plan Italianate villa in England.*

BELOW *Speculative builders as well as architects in the early 19th century produced portfolios of villa designs in every conceivable style. This one was built by the author of one such book, Robert Lugar, in the Isle of Wight.*

styles which Nash was to continue in Park Village, London, and which were later to be one of the charms of Cheltenham, Leamington and other spa towns.

As for Blaise Hamlet, the light-hearted thatched estate village he built in 1803 for a Gloucestershire landowner, it too had its lesson for the more sentimental Victorians (the cottages were named Vine, Oak, Sweet Briar, Jasmine etc). For a new phenomenon had appeared on the scene around the turn of the century – the middle class ex-urbanite. The villa idea had come down in the world since its grand Italian origins, while the *cottage orné* had climbed up. Both were now available on the edge of town to business and professional people, who with the aid of an illustrated handbook

such as Papworth's *Rural Residences* (1818), could pick a design and hire craftsmen to run it up for them.

A digression on glazing bars: the sash windows of the early 18th century had thick white bars that gave them almost the solidity of the surrounding wall. But as the century progressed, better hardwoods enabled the bars to be reduced to as little as a centimetre, and all the elevations of *Vitruvius Britannicus* show the windows as dark voids (though in some very grand houses such as Holkham they were initially gilded). Nash's perspectives show them as painted black, and there is no doubt that this is what best suits his creamy white architecture.

It was through Repton that Nash became the favourite architect of the

Of all the stucco palaces with which Nash lined the circular drive around the Regent's Park, Cumberland Terrace is the grandest. The sculpture-filled pediment has nothing behind it.

future George IV, and in due course the author of the Prince Regent's great scheme for a royal park in St Marylebone linked to his unloved mansion overlooking St James's. Two things mark this extraordinary achievement, which gave to London a new axis so different from the impeccable geometry of Paris. One was the extension of the Woods' language of terrace, crescent and circus to embrace a complete landscape. In this image the architecture does not, as in Bath, dominate; it is seen primarily, in the picturesque mode, as scenery. (Nash was often criticised for his complete lack of interest in the backs of his stucco palaces, though in fact in this he merely followed Georgian precedent. Who knows what happens at the back of Bath's Royal Crescent? It is best not to investigate. Nash did at least take trouble about the return ends of his terraces.)

His second special skill was in improvisation – in itself an aspect of the picturesque. The airy staircase and the two great terraces he devised to replace Carlton House, the Haymarket Theatre closing the vista from St James's Square, the great Quadrant by means of which he handled the side-step of the axis after Piccadilly Circus, the little church steeple by which he turned to good effect the smaller kink at the foot of Portland Place – all these were text-book examples of how the designer can snatch victory out of the jaws of defeat.

In the end he *was* defeated. He could invent stage palaces – even, in the Brighton Pavilion, a fantasy out of the Arabian Nights – but when invited by the King to take on the real thing, Buckingham Palace, he got stage-fright and fell from favour: he was never quite seen as a gentleman.

His contemporary, Sir John Soane, though of equally modest birth, did get his knighthood: he was one of Nature's gentlemen. In every way they were in total contrast. Soane was not clubbable, was easily cast down, and suffered from periods of depression. Like many such introverts, he was a model student, won all the prizes, and in due course made his way to Rome (though not, as was the latest fashion, to Greece). Here he made useful contacts, including a cousin of William Pitt, through whom at the early age of 35 he obtained the appointment of Architect to the Bank of England. Neither Pitt nor anyone else could have guessed that the result was to be a series of domed interiors unlike anything else in Europe.

He has to be thought of in European terms, because his architecture is a deeply personal version of a movement, the neo-classic, which dominated European architecture between 1760 and 1830 and survived (in

To the north-west of the Park, Nash built Park Village, an estate of speculative villas,
no two alike, of which this towered one is among the most attractive.

Glasgow) into the 1870s. This had two strands. The first, as we have seen, was the discovery, and dissemination in England in the 1750s by Stewart and Revett, of the architecture of ancient Greece. Stewart's facade of No 15 St James's Square is an elegant example of the scholarly Ionic, which Soane was to pick up as a pupil of Henry Holland and George Dance. The second was the teaching of the Abbé Laugier, whose *Essay on Architecture*, published in Paris in 1753, threw overboard the whole Vitruvian apparatus of the Orders, with their bases, columns, capitals, entablatures, pediments etc, and advocated an astylar functionalism which derived the Parthenon from the primitive wooden hut. Columns were for supporting roofs, not for mural decoration; pediments were for gables, not for show. In this puritan paradise, Nash was the devil incarnate.

The Laugier philosophy was not calculated to lift the spirits, and such of Soane's early houses as have survived, mostly in grey brick or grey stucco, have an impoverished air. But he single-mindedly pursued his search for new ways of conveying the spirit of classical architecture without its detail. His little lodge at Tyringham is the simplest case, with incised grooves substituting for all ornament. He liked the basic forms of a building, the changes of direction of walls, the resting of roofs on them, to be dramatised by recesses and shadows rather than by projections, and he

*The lodge at Tyringham, Buckinghamshire, and the graceful bridge beyond it, show
Sir John Soane at his most sculptural and abstract. There are no eaves or cornice, and
incised lines take the place of classical mouldings.*

liked to split his shallow domes into segments, or to float them above their supporting walls by inserting narrow strips of glass.

Most of the Bank of England interiors can now, alas, only be imagined from his dramatic perspectives, but when in middle age he came into some money he was able to purchase a site for three houses in Lincoln's Inn Fields, the central one of which is a more graceful Neo-classic design than he ever achieved elsewhere. Within and behind it and extending across the backs of the other two, he slowly created his extraordinary Museum, which is not only a summation of his taste in sculpture and painting but a model of his skill in dramatising interior space. His tiny

domed breakfast room is the smallest architectural masterpiece in England.

Soane's intense imagination went into his lifetime's work in the Bank and the Museum, but one can see at Moggerhanger in Bedfordshire the same feeling for simple masses as in the Tyringham Gateway, and in his (demolished) terrace in Regent Street, the same touch as in Lincoln's Inn Fields – a touch quite beyond the reach of the surrounding Nash ensemble.

In parallel with Soane's lonely journey into abstraction, anonymous Regency builders, too, were working towards a domestic architecture

OPPOSITE *The tiny breakfast room in Soane's Museum in Lincoln's Inn Fields, with its little lantern, refined plasterwork and convex mirrors in the pendentives below the shallow dome, is one of the most masterly interiors in England.* ABOVE *This bow-windowed house in Marlow High Street shows how anonymous Regency builders were able to shed all 'architectural' pretensions, and in the process produce architecture.*

which unaffectedly dispensed with classical ornament, as in the little house in Marlow High Street of 1805, with its characteristic round bays. Simple white houses such as this would soon acquire the pretty black iron balconies and copper 'eyebrows' you will find all over Cheltenham. And the segmental bow windows could be widened, as in Park Lane, London, and in Brighton, to take over the whole frontage of terrace houses.

Meanwhile Neo-classic architecture had a long innings, particularly for public buildings: the British Museum was not completed until 1847, the Harris Library in Preston not until 1893. And it spread rapidly all over the world, from Petersburg to the state capitals of the Middle West, eventually even returning to Athens itself. But for houses it had its limitations. Grecian Ionic worked charmingly for regency villas and for seaside terraces like Brunswick Square in Hove. But the primitive Doric, as in the lodge at Tyringham, could be really grim: the Baring family eventually wrote off as uninhabitable their two Greek Doric country houses in Hampshire. But

up in remote Northumberland two remarkable amateurs pulled it off. I quote from Dr Mordaunt Crook, the authority on the subject:

In the autumn of 1804 Sir Charles Monck Bt (previously Sir Charles Middleton) set off for Athens with his young wife Louisa and spent a protracted honeymoon there. He returned in 1806 with a son named Charles Atticus and a portfolio of architectural drawings. In Athens he had been joined by Sir William Gell. And the designs for a new Belsay – to replace an earlier house of 1614 – were in fact the joint work of Monck and 'Rapid' Gell, with later revisions of detail by John Dobson of Newcastle.

It is an extraordinary house, unique in taking Periclean architecture and decoration into its interior, which is built around a severe Ionic peristyle. Faced with what seems to be an imperishably sharp local limestone, its proportions calculated by Monck, we are told, to three places of decimals,

Scholarly geometry informs the designs of Belsay Hall, here seen at dusk in pure elevation.

it exemplifies in its setting an extreme case of the juxtaposition of the rational and the romantic which was the essence of the Picturesque. But one wonders what young Dobson was allowed to contribute. The best, and probably the only architect in the North of England, he was to go on to build the superb classical Grey Street in Newcastle, all in a rich tawny stone, which made London's Regent Street look cheap, and finally in what seems another age, Newcastle's grand Central Station.

Neo-classicism was inspired by travel writers exploring Europe, just as Adam, Burlington, Wren, Inigo Jones and Smythson had been. Not so the Gothic Revival, whose inspiration was solely English. But it took longer to take off, and Georgian Gothic had a longer lifespan, because the scholarly spade-work was not done until the 19th century. John Britton's exhaustive and exhausting surveys (county by county, much of them done on foot) of the architectural heritage of England and Wales, and then of the Gothic cathedrals, began to appear in 1800, in beautiful and accurate engravings, and continued into the 1840s. They were eye-openers, as epoch-making as the work of Piper, Pevsner and Betjeman in our own century. But it took more than the drawings of Britton's artists to transform the Gothic Revival into Revivalism – a passionate enterprise quite different in spirit from the cool Grecian. The polemic that did the trick was the publication in 1836 of a book called *Contrasts*, by the 24-year-old Augustus Welby Pugin. This was because it caught a new mood in England and indeed in Europe.

CHAPTER 7

Serious Gothic

A Victorian photograph of Highclere Castle, Hampshire.

WHETHER YOU LOVED OR HATED HIM, NAPOLEON HAD aroused an excitement in Europe that his fall could not put to rest. The sense of drama, of living through enormous events, so grandiosely conveyed by Thomas Hardy's verse-play *The Dynasts*, the awakening of nationalism, the possibility of rebuilding society from top to bottom – was all this to be forgotten in the restored monarchies? Stendhal, Balzac and Flaubert in their different ways conveyed a feeling of disillusion, frustration and contempt for the bourgeois obsession with money. British writers like Southey, Cobbett and Carlyle expressed the same nostalgia in overtly political terms. To these romantics, a bad king or a mad one was better value than dull ones like Louis Philippe or William IV, the latter aptly reflected, they thought, in the endless Greek temple fronts of 'stylophiles' (lovers of columns) like

Wilkins and Smirke. But whereas in France the cry was 'Back to the Future!' – the glorious future promised by Bonaparte – in England it was, characteristically, 'Back to the Past!' – back to the truly British, the native and noble Gothic that (they persuaded themselves) owed nothing to foreign influences.

The cult of the Middle Ages – the return to Camelot, as Mark Girouard has described it – although it later penetrated to Central Europe, had to happen in Britain, because of the survival here of a firmly territorial, paternalist and comparatively accessible aristocracy, continually refreshed by new blood since Tudor times. Consequently the emotional reaction against Benthamite Utilitarianism, comparable with the 1980s reaction against the Welfare State, could find a focus (bogus though it may often have been) in Chivalry, in the image of the knight in shining armour

PRECEDING PAGES *The monstrous, marvellous pile of Salvin's Harlaxton Manor near Grantham has been described as 'Vanbrugh translated into Jacobethan Revival'.*
OPPOSITE *The Gothic silhouette of Toddington Manor in Gloucestershire rises behind trees planted on its bare plateau when work started on the great house.*

*Lord Sudeley, amateur architect, started work on the central block at Toddington
in 1820, using the Collegiate Gothic style which was later to be adopted by Barry
and Pugin for the Palace of Westminster.*

riding about doing good. The cult of the English gentleman, well-born, generous, imperturbable, was born. Disraeli's Young England movement was the first manifestation of Tory radicalism, more adventurous than the prosperous Whigs dared to be, which was to survive well into the 20th century. By the 1830s it was the middle-aged who clung to Neo-classicism; the young were Goths.

Pugin was an artist, not a writer: his father had come from France to work as one of Nash's illustrators. The contrasts he depicted were between an imaginary 15th-century city, all gabled houses, fretted palaces, and dreaming spires, and a typical Midland manufacturing town, with its tiers of

warehouses, flat roofs, stucco terraces, boxy churches, smoking chimneys and up-to-date gaols: God displaced by Mammon. In the words of the most ardent medievalist of them all, Kenelm Digby (also a Catholic convert):

Remark too that the religious, civil and military architecture of those ages rose aloft and struck the eyes, unlike the modern which is flat and levelled, like the ranks of our social state. Chateaubriand asks, 'Will our age leave such a testimony in its passage?' We have no longer the faith which moved so many stones. We raise exchanges, bazaars, coffee houses, club-houses.

*Kiddington Hall near Oxford is a comparatively modest example of Barry's so-called
Italianate style of the mid-century, with its heavy cornice and plate-glass windows.*

As for the architects, they were no longer artists: they were a superior kind of tradesman. One convenient catalogue, Richard Brown's *Domestic Architecture*, published in 1841, offered the following styles: *Cottage Orné*, Tudor, Stuart, Florentine, Flemish, Pompeian, Venetian, Swiss, French Chateau, Egyptian, Grecian, Roman, Anglo-Grecian, Anglo-Italian, Persian, Chinese, Burmese, Oriental, Morisco-Gothic, Norman, Lancastrian, Plantagenet, and Palladian.

That Gothic already had high prestige when *Contrasts* was published was proved by the announcement in the same year that the new Palace of Westminster was to be in the Gothic or Elizabethan style – a stipulation that could have been made in no other country in 1836. It was a demonstration both of the medieval mystique surrounding the institution of Parliament and of the essential Englishness, as it was thought, of these styles. The competition winner, in fact, Charles Barry, was no Goth (except for churches), and wisely engaged Pugin to gothicise his basically classical scheme in a manner which created a masterpiece and occupied both men

for the rest of their lives. Among the assessors of the competition was Lord Sudeley, who had himself designed and been building since 1819 a great house, Toddington Manor, on his Gloucestershire estate. Like that other amateur of Gothic, Newdigate at Arbury, Sudeley was still too conditioned by classical symmetry to escape from it. But his great house is still a remarkable essay in the Oxford collegiate style of the 15th century, widely imitated in the early 19th, but seldom with such care and conviction. At a glance it could almost be a model for the winning design for Westminster, and no doubt it predisposed Lord Sudeley to vote for Barry and Pugin, although there is no evidence that either of the winners ever set eyes on Toddington (nor would Pugin have considered it true Gothic if he had).

With one possible exception, the recasing by Charles Barry of Lord Carnarvon's Georgian house at Highclere near Newbury, the Barry/Pugin collaboration bore no fruit in their separate practices, or in the country houses designed by either. Barry's remained firmly classical, in the Italianate manner he had first demonstrated in the Travellers' Club in London.

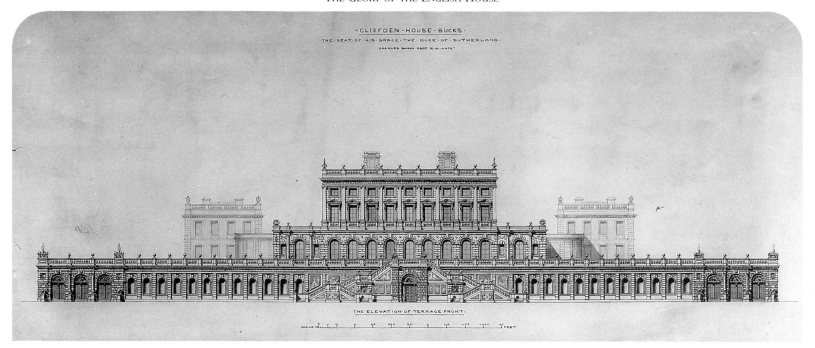

For Cliveden on its wooded escarpment above the Thames, rebuilt for the Duke of Sutherland after a fire in 1850, Barry used a restrained Jonesian manner to suit the 17th-century terraces on which it stands. OPPOSITE *Alton Castle in Staffordshire was a ruin when A. W. Pugin was employed by the Earl of Shrewsbury to rebuild it in 1847. He allowed the shape of the rock to determine the shape of the building.*

Almost all were rebuilds to meet the inflated needs of the early Victorian household, and often, as at Kingston Lacy in Dorset, they overloaded a restrained Restoration design. *Portes-cochères* might be attached, water-towers or campaniles erected, colonnades, *parterres* and statutary extended into the previously sheep-mown parklands left by Brown or Repton. By the mid-century, the Barry style becomes more heavily Victorian, with broad plate-glass windows and bulky cornices and balustrades. Kiddington, a prettily situated house near Oxford, is a good example. But he could still, most conspicuously at Cliveden, design with some elegance. This great house was another rebuild, after a fire, and here he could take advantage of the spectacular platform, high above the Thames, which the Duke of Buckingham had contrived in the 1660s. Two centuries later Barry's classical mansion, in a rather congested Jonesian manner, crowning tier on tier of balustraded terraces, rose above a mature landscape in which French formality and English opportunism were happily married. In this case the *porte-cochère* and the remarkable Baroque campanile are by later architects.

Poor Pugin in his short life, committed to the heavy burden of translating into his obsessive Gothic the completely unmedieval requirements of the Catholic gentry, had it much less easy. He believed 'that there should be no features about a building which are not necessary for convenience, construction or propriety; second, that all ornament should consist of the necessary construction of the building' – sentiments that anticipate William Morris and his circle in the next generation. But he was too deeply in love with Gothic ornament and its rich coloration to practise

what he preached. Perhaps his most attractive domestic work is the comparatively modest castle/folly he built for Lord Shrewsbury at Alton. Perched on its rock above a dark forest, this Wagnerian scenario gave Pugin the chance he wanted to allow the different elements of a building to come together as if by accident, by physical necessity, rather than by design – a flouting of picturesque theory which produces a magically picturesque effect.

Despite these comparative successes, both on exceptionally dramatic sites, Barry's best work was in the heart of London, not in his country houses, and Pugin's in his churches. We are entering a period in which private houses cease, for a time, to be the main interest of architects. The masterpieces of Victorian architecture are its churches and its great constructions in iron and glass. In the domestic field, in town and country alike, the Victorian age is as remarkable, as notorious, for what it destroyed as for what it built. It had a contempt for everything built since the time of Queen Anne which was quite unprecedented, and it had the resources to act on this. In London, the whole red brick City disappeared, and the Georgian quarters east of it, invaded by an army of workers displaced off the land, declined into slums; while in every provincial city new public buildings arose which cocked a snook at their Georgian environment. Charles Dickens had this to say about Georgian houses:

horrors that came into existence under some wrong-headed person in some wrong-headed time, still demanding the blind admiration of all ensuing generations.

Alton Castle, towering above its wooded rock, is best seen (like most deliberately picturesque castles) from a distance.

Since the completion of the first iron bridge at Coalbrookdale in 1779 the industrial revolution had leapt ahead – railways slicing through the soft parklike landscape and wrapping their tentacles around the hearts of cities. Buildings put on their black coats, and so did men, topping them off with the tall hats they were to wear in all public places, indoors and out, to the end of the century. For architecture, the two key materials were structural cast iron and sheet glass (the first polished sheet appeared in 1838), which were to make possible masterpieces like the Palm House at Kew and the Crystal Palace, as well as the ubiquitous Victorian conservatory, but which were also to inject into the minds of architects their own version of the schizophrenia which was to haunt the Victorian imagination.

For the fact was that the imagery which Pugin tried to hard to respond to was literary rather than visual.

Thus Keats:

> A casement high and triple-arch'd there was,
> All garlanded with carven imag'ries
> Of fruits, and flowers, and bunches of knot-grass,
> And diamonded with panes of quaint device,
> Innumerable of stains and splendid dyes,
> As are the tiger-Moth's deep-damask'd wings;
> And in the midst, 'mong thousand heraldries,
> And twilight saints, and dim emblazonings,
> A shielded scutcheon blush'd with blood of queens
> And kings.

and Tennyson:

> Likewise the deepset windows, stained and traced,
> Burned, like slow flaming crimson fires,
> From shadowed grots or arches interlaced,
> And topped with frostlike spires.
>
> Up in the towers I placed great bells that swung,
> Moved of themselves with silver sound:
> And with choice paintings of wise men I hung
> The royal dais round.

OPPOSITE *Milton Ernest near Bedford (1856) is by William Butterfield and is in his mature style, with its almost painfully sharp roofs and dormers and his characteristic 'cut-out' stone windows.*

These dreams, this misty, magic world conjured up in the *Idylls of the King* – how were you to *build* it? The poet's uncle, Charles Tennyson d'Eyncourt (the name taken from a shadowy ancestor of his wife) actually tried. In 1836 (that same momentous year) he started work to transform Bayons Manor in Lincolnshire into the magic castle of his dreams. Probably, in its heyday, when Charles entertained a hundred guests in the Great Hall, the whole enterprise seemed just as bogus as many a modern fake medieval banquet. But when Bayons fell into ruin and remained buried in cobwebs and undergrowth until its demolition in 1965, it must at last have looked like the legendary palace of the Sleeping Beauty.

This was the trouble: the romantic dream was in hopeless conflict with the facts of 19th-century technology. Instead of magic casements it offered flawless plate glass, instead of ancient stones, machine-made bricks of an unprecedented hardness, instead of candles casting moving shadows, gas-lighting. For the first time in history, but not the last, men – some men – looked upon their brilliant new inventions not with pride but with dismay. Comically symbolic of the state of things was the famous Eglinton Tournament of 1839, where 12 Tory knights in full armour, each leading brilliant retinues, were mercilessly rained off just as they were about to begin the joust and had to leave the field under golf umbrellas. Tragically symbolic of the underlying sense of loss was Matthew Arnold's poem *Dover Beach*, echoing down to our day.

In fact, with the more serious and politically fraught 1840s, the sillier aspects of fancy dress medievalism went out of fashion, and firm believers in the validity of Gothic principles set out to adapt them to modern materials, which was of course the only sensible way forward. In France Viollet-le-Duc analysed Gothic architecture not as a style but as a rational system of construction working logically forward from precedent to precedent – the very synthesis which 19th-century engineers made so brilliantly but 19th-century architects were too bemused by detail to attempt. And in England his exact contemporary, William Butterfield, a very different character, used modern materials in a version of Gothic as flamboyantly personal as Vanbrugh's Baroque. But he was not flamboyant: he was one of those shy and austere Victorian bachelors, attended all his life (he died in 1900) by a faithful married couple, and content to consort with a tiny group of slightly crackpot High Churchmen. He built nearly a hundred churches, and as our first Brutalist (but by no means, among the Victorians, our last) his influence was profound. This is why (and because I

like it) I include his only country house – Milton Ernest in Bedfordshire, built in the mid 1850s for a London business man who had married the sister of the architect.

Milton Ernest has all the features of High Victorian Gothic – the elaborate asymmetry (with consequent effects on the cost of maintaining the complicated crested roofs), the tall chimneys, the painfully sharp gables. Specifically Butterfieldian is the clash of projections on the entrance front, the multi-coloured brick decoration, and the flat windows, as though cut out of smooth slabs of stone, something Pugin could never have contemplated. Cottages in the village, red brick with traditional white-painted casements, show that Butterfield was capable of unbending on occasion, as he did in many of his modest clergy houses. The stripped-down Butterfield manner in fact spread all over the country: it was inexpensive and appropriate for professional people. When Oxford dons were allowed to marry in the 1870s it was used for a number of houses in north Oxford, and none of the great Victorian cities are without excellent, if somewhat forbidding, examples.

But while domesticated, scaled down Gothic made some impact in the leafier suburbs of Bradford and Birmingham, it never seemed sensible wear for the long terraces which were still the only way developers could see of accommodating the upper-middle class in the high-cost estates of West London. Consequently a gulf, which had not existed in the 18th century, had opened up between urban houses, Neo-classic and orderly, and country houses, romantic and escapist, although occasionally urban builder/designers like Thomas Cubitt and Decimus Burton got a country house to do (even, eventually, the Prince Consort's great villa, Osborne, on the Isle of Wight). In London, as development spread beyond Cubitt's finely built streets and squares in Belgravia and Pimlico into the remoter reaches of Kensington and Bayswater, the stucco terraces become thicker and taller with the increased wealth of their purchasers. But well into the 1860s they remained classical in the so-called Italianate manner introduced by Barry, with an increased use of round-headed windows. Over-dressed and often vulgar though they are, all these streets are now listed as of historic interest, which one must suppose they are. But their architectural interest is minimal: architects had long since ceased to design them.

Out in the country, with the mid-century, we enter the age of the Victorian monsters or, more kindly, the prodigy houses of the 19th century. Unlike the great houses of the Elizabethans and the Georgians,

Looking upwards to the roof of the staircase at Harlaxton is a truly surrealist experience, with its gigantic ornament and dream-like perspectives.

these enormous mansions were not built as demonstrations of wealth, culture and architectural expertise, open to the public and widely discussed. Instead they were built as solutions for an immensely complex social problem: how to house a rich family with many children, guests or relatives staying for weeks on end, weekend parties bringing their own servants, and a domestic heirarchy from governesses and tutors down to scullery maids, in such a way that none of these groups of people, which together might add up to a hundred or more, got in one another's way. At the same time provision must be made for bathrooms, waste disposal, central heating and gas supplies, and the flues from coal fireplaces in every remote

room had to be brought together in groups. If one looks at a typical plan by the Scot William Burn, thought to be the most skilful of problem solvers if not the most exciting of architects, one can see that classical symmetry was not simply no longer wanted, it was unattainable if he was to meet these incredibly complex needs. The result was a building which, whatever its style, might or might not present an orderly front, but trailed off at the back into a maze of service quarters.

The question of style, nevertheless, was the first to arise when (or indeed before) you engaged an architect. In simple terms, you had a choice of three, and your choice would be determined by your background and

A spectacular chandelier lights the Hall at Harlaxton and its shiny Tudorbethan panelling. At the end is a richly carved pseudo-Renaissance marble screen. NEXT PAGES *Harlaxton, seen through its entrance gates, blazes with the lights of late-night students.*

taste. For the Whig aristocracy and for the rich with London houses, the Italianate of Barry or Burn (who could in fact do you anything) was still seen as the soundest investment, although of diminishing chic as the century wore on. For the remoter country gentry with strong Christian principles and an equally strong sense of tradition, the right thing was the muscular Gothic of architects like Scott and Teulon. And for the less secure there was always the pastiche Jacobethan of Blore and Salvin. (If you were really brave, of course, Salvin, or later Burges, could create for you a splendidly convincing castle: castles never quite ceased to be built even as late as 1930.)

These were all highly professional men, members of the Institute of British Architects (founded in 1834), with large practices. (Lord Sudeley's Toddington was the last prodigy house to be designed by an amateur.) But one could never be sure whether their buildings, which would certainly be expensive, would turn out hideous or magnificent – or indeed how to judge. Teulon in particular, a reclusive and difficult artist, could go either way. His additions to Chadwell in Norfolk, for example, transformed a dullish Jacobethan house of the 1840s into something sensational. And if Chadwell is sensational, what is one to say of Harlaxton? Salvin's design of the early 1830s, all in Ancaster stone, is of course pastiche Jacobean, and

The entrance front of Harlaxton is a blend of Montacute, Burghley and Hengrave.

readers will be able to identify some of its sources, English and French; but, in a way never again to be achieved by this architect, it seems to transcend them and attain a higher level of inspiration, fruitless to analyse. Again, one is reminded of Vanbrugh, not only in the high drama of the silhouette, here pale against dark woodlands, but in the gateposts and garden walls, executed in fact by William Burn but almost certainly to Salvin's designs. The interior is equally extraordinary, most of all the surrealist staircase hall, which Cocteau and Dali could scarcely have bettered.

We cannot move (with some relief) out of the high Victorian decades without some mention of its two commanding figures, John Ruskin and Sir George Gilbert Scott. Ruskin published *The Seven Lamps of Architecture* in 1849. His passionate eloquence still resonates. Idealisation of the Middle Ages, demand for structural honesty, moral contempt for mass produced ornament, all these follow Pugin and anticipate William Morris. Ruskin's special loves, however, are for carving, particularly from nature, and for the delicacy of Venetian Gothic and its use of coloured masonry. Even Scott, worldliest, busiest and most successful of high Victorian architects, was persuaded to send the sculptors of his Gothic capitals out into the hedgerows. A house like Kelham near Nottingham shows the remarkable result, but is in other respects too unpleasant for inclusion here. Scott, the

Ettington Park in Warwickshire was built for the Shirleys around 1860 in the 'Early Pointed' style. Its banded polychromatic stonework and sculptured reliefs show the influence of John Ruskin.

great builder of government offices, clubs, hotels, and, of course, churches, was too grand to build houses that worked. Those curious to get an idea of Kelham need travel no further than the Euston Road in London and look up at the St Pancras Hotel.

A comparatively modest house in Warwickshire by an obscure Welsh pupil of A. W. Pugin called Pritchard comes as close as any (and few do) to demonstrating the influence of the *Seven Lamps*. Ettington was built for the Shirleys over the same years as Chadwell. Though scarcely Venetian, it is elaborately carved with subjects related to the history of Sherwood Forest, in which the family had held land since before the Norman Conquest. It is also prettily polychromatic in the manner of Butterfield and has a lightness of touch of which he was seldom capable.

CHAPTER 8

Old English

Norman Shaw's Cragside in Northumberland (1870).

THE HIGH VICTORIAN HOUSE AMPLY ENSHRINED ITS OWNERS, their oppressed, upholstered ladies, earnestly applied to good works, and the solemn, or bigoted, or hearty Victorian husbands and fathers who were to become the butt of the great succession of novels that runs from Eliot's *Middlemarch* to Butler's *The Way of All Flesh*. If ever a period's life-style called for a reaction it was this one. But the transition from the world of Dickens to the world of Oscar Wilde, unlike earlier changes of taste, was effected not by aristocratic patrons but by the new metropolitan upper-middle class, unostentatious, comfortably rich, and leisured enough to study and admire the work of artists as various as Morris and de Morgan, Whistler and Burne-Jones. Muscular Gothic, dramatising the struggle of mid-Victorian businessmen to earn wealth and respect, was about the last thing wanted by the relaxed, witty

and agnostic aesthetes of the new generation. Eclectic in their tastes, they were in no hurry to pursue the old search for a style worthy of the 19th century. But of course they could not help acquiring one of their own, as unmistakable as any of the past.

This was to be called, by them, quite misleadingly, 'Queen Anne'. If Walter Scott was the literary godfather of Victorian Gothic, W. M. Thackeray was the protagonist of 'Queen Anne'. Unlike his contemporary Charles Dickens, who hated Georgian architecture, Thackeray, a much more visual person, set his best known novel in this period. And near the end of his life he built himself one of the first red brick mansions in Kensington, opposite the Palace, in a style crudely reminiscent of Thomas Archer, and too Baroque for the younger men of the 1860s to wish to pursue. For them, and in particular for William Morris's architect, Philip Webb, the less style

PRECEDING PAGES *Deanery Garden on the Thames at Sonning, by Edwin Lutyens (1902), is in the Old English manner introduced by Norman Shaw.* OPPOSITE *Arts-and-crafts timber work of 1893, on a gable of Wightwick Manor in Staffordshire.*

The architect E. W. Godwin's sketch is of the romantic timber-framed shooting-box, Beauvale, which he built for Earl Cowper in 1871-73 in Sherwood Forest near Nottingham.

the better. Webb admired Butterfield's simple red brick and sash windowed clergy houses and wished to design in what Frank Lloyd Wright would later call an 'organic' manner, eschewing symmetry, rejecting the discipline of the Orders, and emulating the casual assemblage of steep roofs, great chimneys, and windows placed where they were needed – all in what he thought of as the quintessentially English tradition. The studio house at 14 Holland Park Road, London, designed in 1864 for the artist Val Prinsep, is one of the earliest examples. This of course was not Queen Anne at all – not at all what Wren and his successors, to whom symmetry was second nature, had been after. Paired sash windows, one of Butterfield's less attractive inventions, are a particularly untraditional device.

There is something ham-fisted in the surviving English houses of high-minded Webb, and I do not love any of them enough to include them in this book.* The opposite is true of his brilliant contemporaries, Norman Shaw and W. E. Nesfield. Both these men, born in the 1830s and in loose partnership from 1871, represented the new breed of architect who had not, as in the previous century, come up from the building trade, but were members themselves of the class for whom they built. Nesfield was an Etonian, Shaw a member of a Liverpool shipping dynasty; both were ebulliently self-confident, with the artist's flair rather than the craftsman's. They inaugurate a period, to be crowned by the work of Lutyens, when what would be 'fun' became once more a design criterion.

At this point we need to make a distinction between two strands in this pseudo-vernacular movement. The first, labelled by the Victorian architectural taxonomist Charles Eastlake 'Old English', and adopted at once by Shaw and Nesfield to describe their country work, was pioneered by George Devey in his rambling black and white half-timbered country houses for the very rich, of which Ascott, one of the Rothschild houses in Buckinghamshire, is characteristic. Shaw's Old English masterpiece is undoubtedly Cragside, which transcends anything in this style Devey, or Nesfield, were capable of. This great house built for the Tyneside armaments magnate, Sir William Armstrong, is perched like a German eyrie on a rock escarpment commanding miles of Northumbrian moorland. It is now somewhat buried among conifers and rhododendrons, from which only glimpses can be seen of its complex and gradually assembled composition of stone and half timber. Shaw's original drawing conveys it best.

At Cragside, Shaw's use of half-timbering (quite alien to the locality, of course) is minimal and ornamental, as in all his houses. The same goes for his contemporary E. W. Godwin. Godwin, like his friend William Burges, was a romantic and bohemian Goth, entirely without Christian affiliations, and when in 1871 the 7th Earl Cowper commissioned him to design a forest lodge, wholly for fun, in the midst of what remained of Sherwood Forest, he was living with the actress Ellen Terry and hard up; so the job was a godsend. Beauvale is a tower house, steep roofed, pyramidal in composition and more Old Burgundian than Old English. From its tower windows (as Mark Girouard writes), 'a lady of Shalott should have been looking out over the tree-tops'.

---

*Unfortunately what must have been the most attractive, Rounton Grange in Yorkshire and Joldwynds in Surrey, are gone.

The garden side of Wightwick Manor is a fine essay in Victorian carpentry, although the hard red Ruabon bricks (so hated by his successors) ensure it could not be mistaken for the real thing.

In the end, of course, all that remained of Old English in the popular mind was the half-timbering; Devey carried the day. Wightwick Manor in Staffordshire was built in two stages in the 1880s and 1890s for a Wolverhampton business man, employing a local architect who specialised in the elaborate half-timbered 'restoration' of old Chester. To those who have studied Ockwells, Little Moreton and Pitchford its sources are obvious, as is its far more careful interest in those ancestors than Devey bothered with. The interior, with its pretty stained glass by Kempe, its rich 'Jacobean' ceilings and friezes, its Morris papers and embroideries, and its blue and white china collection, shows how far into the provinces the artistic taste of the '90s penetrated. But with the turn of the century the style slid steadily downhill into the world of 1920s public houses and Stockbroker's Tudor, and the pathetic travesties of the speculative builders.*

---

*I was born in a Tudorbethan house built by my grandfather in 1884 on the edge of Windsor Forest, complete with timbered gables, tile-hung walls, latticed windows, brick paved garden paths and wrought iron gates, pergolas, and Renaissance wellheads. It was much admired by the Kaiser, who must have heard of Muthesius' influential book *Das Englische Haus* and asked for the designs which, he thought, would fit admirably into the environs of Potsdam. It always astonished us that a man considered to be of refined taste could have built such a ye olde mansion and then filled it with Louis Seize furniture.

The interior of the Hall at Wightwick shows its affinity with Ockwells. The glass of 1893 is by Kempe, who worked with William Morris on the interiors generally.

The second strand, 'Queen Anne' (though its inventors would have preferred 'free-classic' and Osbert Lancaster in his 1938 *Pillar to Post* called it 'Pont Street Dutch'), was essentially urban or suburban and started life in London.

By the 1840s the London-type terrace house had ceased to be built in provincial cities, prosperous people preferring to move well away from the mills into detached villas in Edgbaston, or Allerton, or Moss Side. But in London it spread rapidly north and west, the houses becoming steadily taller as middle-class families grew and servants multiplied. The tallest of all were in respectable South Kensington, in a debased stucco style developed from Barry's Italianate, which its builders would no doubt describe as 'free classic'. It can be amply studied in Queen's Gate and parts west. But also in Queen's Gate are some very different houses, two of them by Norman Shaw. These are in red brick, one of them unquestionably 'Queen Anne' but the other (No 196) in an even redder shade of red and in a much more elaborate gabled style, with a great deal of moulded brickwork, mullioned windows, and leaded lights, which can best be described as Tudor Renaissance.

Shaw's client here was J. P. Heseltine, stockbroker, collector and amateur artist, and as such typical of the artistic people who enthusiastically adopted 'Queen Anne'. Another such was George Howard of Castle Howard, whose enormous mansion of 1867 in Palace Green (alongside Thackeray's) shows Webb in transition from Butterfield's influence to Shaw's. Five years later Lowther Lodge (now the Royal Geographical Society), facing Kensington Gardens, shows the far greater consistency, panache and sense of enjoyment the style had achieved.

By the 1870s the inflated art of the Royal Academy summer shows brought splendid fortunes to its practitioners. A good place to study their studio-houses is Melbury Road, described by Sir Hugh Casson as the Victorian equivalent of Beverly Hills, where *inter alia* there are characteristic houses by Burges and Shaw and a glorious polychromatic house by Halsey Ricardo. A more sedate collection of Victorian mansions lines Kensington Palace Gardens. Here are all the styles from 1840s Tudor, through Barry and his followers in both the Elizabethan and Italianate modes, to a handsome collection of Shavian red brick embassies where the dead straight avenue opens up into Palace Green. Security is high in this privileged enclave, so beware of inspecting any one building too closely.

This Dutch-style facade in Cadogan Square is by Ernest George, in whose office Lutyens worked as an assistant. The riotous use of terracotta was a speciality of that architect. OPPOSITE *Swan House on Chelsea Embankment was completed by Norman Shaw in 1875, and is one of his most subtle designs. The 'Sparrowes' oriel windows were to be a favourite device of his.*

This was all great fun, but detached houses for the very rich were not the real problem, which was to revitalise the terrace house. For this, two conspicuous opportunities occurred in the mid-1870s – the creation of the Chelsea Embankment looking across the River to Battersea Park, and the decision of Lord Cadogan to develop the Hans Town estate west of Sloane Street (for which, a sign of the times, red brick would be mandatory). What emerged were not true terraces at all, but variegated row houses reminiscent of Lubeck or Amsterdam, some elegant, some stodgy, some actively eccentric. In both locations the most elegant, as usual, are Norman Shaw's, the stodgiest the work of the Scotsman J. J. Stephenson, one of the pioneers of the style. The most eccentric are those of Ernest George, whose Flemish terracotta houses in Cadogan Square and Mount Street fathered a whole brood of similar architecture in Mayfair and Chelsea, culminating in the vulgarity of the enormous Harrods department store. Of them all, Shaw's symmetrical Swan House on Chelsea Embankment (1875) is the most appealing to our eyes, with its slim and elegant drawing room windows on the second floor, his beloved 'Sparrowe's House' oriels tucked in below, and the refreshing (to us) absence of moulded brickwork.

For various reasons, not least its high cost, the 'Queen Anne' movement in the West End had spent itself by the end of the century. This was just as well. It was never really suited to terrace building, since it depended for its success on variety of design, as it had in the Netherlands and the Baltic, and could never have emulated the classless adaptability of the Georgian terrace. Its heavy reds looked well among green trees, but were unbearably oppressive in an ordinary London street, for which the houses were too tall as well as too dark. In fact these houses were too tall from the start, witness Philip Webb's house for George Howard in Palace Green, which so dwarfs Thackeray's little mansion alongside. Their ceiling heights, proclaiming wealth, were out of scale with residential London, and would before long be out of reach financially too.

In suburbia, as first in Bedford Park, in the commuter counties opened up by the railways, on the banks of the rural Thames, and at the seaside, it was a different story. Here, suitably scaled down, the new style was a smash hit. It seemed to be a game that all could play, requiring no expertise. In the nationwide riot of cheerful vulgarity that ensued, the work of the original protagonists seems notably restrained. Shaw's Merrist Wood in leafy Surrey, with its high windows, tile-hanging, and

*Merrist Wood in leafy Surrey is a modest commuter's house by Shaw, and shows his
liberal use of white-painted woodwork. The huge oriel was to be imitated in oak by
Lutyens at Deanery Gardens and at Plumpton.*

sparkling white paint, is one of a group of such quite modest commuter houses.

But for the country house in the traditional sense 'Queen Anne' was handicapped by its *nouveau riche* associations; and in any case by the 1890s country landowners were feeling the pinch of the agricultural depression. Two architects, Stephenson and Nesfield, did make brave attempts to adapt the style to the scale of the great house. Stephenson's Ken Hill near the north Norfolk coast is in fact not a great house at all, but a small one given dignity by being modelled on a medieval hall-house, with dominant hall windows flanked by two asymmetrical wings, and then lifted like a pal-ladian mansion to *piano-nobile* level, with service rooms below – a rare mixture of traditions that works extremely well. Unusually, Stephenson here eschews his beloved red brick and uses the rich brown local stone.

For five years Nesfield had worked somewhat in the shadow of Shaw, as once had Hawksmoor in the shadow of Vanbrugh, though he took no part in the Pont Street Dutch exercise. It seems to have been Nesfield who introduced the sunflower motif which became the signature symbol of the 'Queen Anne' style. His little lodge in Kew Gardens, with its enormous chimney, although it was built as early as 1866, is much more Edwardian than mid-Victorian in feeling, and clearly influenced the later work of

*A rare country house by J. J. Stephenson, who made his name on the Cadogan Estate
in London, Ken Hill in Norfolk (1888) is built of brown stone on the model of the
East Anglian hall-house.*

Norman Shaw. And there survives, buried now in the suburban fringes of East London, his Manor House at Loughton in Essex, an evocation of the late 17th century translated into the language of the late 19th. This too has a quite un-Victorian lightness of touch which was to turn out to be the movement's first legacy to the 20th century.

The second is the free plan. The informal grouping of rooms was an invention of Nash and the Picturesque, but done by him more for external effect than internal convenience. The high Victorians had pursued it on a vaster scale, but the rooms themselves, whether Classic or Gothic, tended to be conventional in shape, and so cluttered up with occasional chairs, draped tables, musical instruments, house plants and bibelots of every kind that their shapes scarcely registered at all. It was the Shaw generation who, partly by clearing a lot of the junk away under Japanese influences and partly by devising and enjoying fireside inglenooks, window seats, and romantic low-ceilinged embrasures of all kinds, liberated internal planning from the convention of rooms altogether, and led directly to Frank Lloyd Wright's interiors in the USA, and eventually in England.

By the 1890s, Norman Shaw had become, his friends thought, excessively grand and baroque, building in that manner an enormous red and white country house in Dorset for the Duke of Portland and an equally

177

OPPOSITE *This little lodge in Kew Gardens, with its enormous chimney, was designed by W. E. Nesfield and built as early as 1866. Its white-painted cornice and large dormers influenced the work of Shaw.* ABOVE *Annesley Lodge in Hampstead was built by Charles Annesley Voysey for his father. Its rough plaster, corner buttresses and long ranges of square-mullioned windows are the marks of his rather puritanical style.*

enormous hotel in London in the middle of Nash's Regent Street quadrant. But then, in the eyes of the young, his generation had never really understood William Morris's message, nor earned by dedicated study and restraint the Old English label it had laid claim to.

The launch of the Arts and Crafts Society in 1888 was the signal for a new attempt to recover for the individual designer, or better still for the group or guild of like-minded artist/craftsmen, the integrity which, in Morris's view, had been swamped by Victorian vulgarity and mass production. This little group of high-minded designers, led by C. R. Ashbee (1863-1942), who worked most tirelessly, first in London and later in the Cotswolds, to put Morris's Guild Socialism into practice, was by definition anti-populist and therefore unpopular. Shy, socialist, pacifist, 'simple-lifers' were suspect from the start to the men with money, and well into the 20th century were caricatured as the bearded, sandalled denizens of Letchworth and Welwyn Garden City. Their loveliest work is a small group of churches where they could combine their skills to best effect.

Their London houses have to be sought out – a pair by Ashbee in Cheyne Walk, Chelsea (38-39), an elegant one by Mackmurdo surviving at the back end of Peter Jones department store, a small group off Mortimer Street, and three in Hans Road (12-16) alongside Harrods, of which the

OPPOSITE *This is a measured drawing of Munstead Wood, Lutyens's first sizeable house, built for his formidable patron Miss Jekyll in 1896-97 in the local Bargate stone. Its design anticipates the more sophisticated Tigbourne.*

two best are Voysey's. Charles Annesley Voysey is the best known of these architects, because his plain white roughcast houses with their buttressed corners and long ranges of square-mullioned windows could be seen (wholly against his own intentions) as precursors of modernism. The charming L-shaped one he built for his father in Platts Lane, West Hampstead, survives externally, somewhat enveloped in trees, and one can see how influential it was to be, despite Voysey's withdrawn nature, and how fittingly it embraced the designer's wallpapers and chintzes and simple oak furniture from Heals, the first store to market it. Of his few and modest country houses, Broadleys (1898) overlooking Windermere, with its three round bays and sweeping roofs, is entirely without the mannerisms that separate us from Victorian 'Queen Anne' and consign it to history: it seems unaffectedly contemporary with ourselves.

This is not true of most of the architecture and artifacts of the Arts and Crafts movement. Medieval in inspiration even when most ardently styleless, its 'Celtic' curves and tendrils and its love of wrought iron often assimilate it to continental Art Nouveau – a relationship which this consciously British group hotly denied. Certainly it seemed to contemporaries irremediably arty, and to some rather younger Edwardian architects like Ernest Newton, Detmar Blow, and Guy Dawber it still smelt strongly of 'Chelsea'. Their solution was to be pure vernacular pastiche, either in the brick and tile and rough oak of *Old West Surrey**, or in the random rubble and Stonesfield slates of the Cotswolds, with a great display of the bare bones of the house – oak beams, interior masonry, unpainted lime plaster. There are villages like Hambledon and Sapperton where you simply cannot tell 1610 and 1910 apart.

Meanwhile, in the world of the speculators, large and small, the first decade of the new century was the free-for-all of all time. Anything went. For the last 50 years the population explosion had been their goldmine, so that whereas in the early 19th century all building was architecture, in the early 20th the search for a piece of architecture was for a needle in a haystack. The collapse of the traditional balance between town and country was not just an environmental disaster; it was a social disgrace. Elitist architects were made to feel they fiddled while Rome burned. Their steadfast opponent was W. R. Lethaby, not the Arts and Crafts movement's best architect but its most far-sighted thinker, who wrote that he 'did not

believe in genius one bit, nor anything else abnormal'. He 'wanted the commonplace'. 'Art should be everywhere. It cannot exist in isolation or man thick; it must be a thousand men thick.'

It is impossible to draw any line giving architecture a superior status to building that does not result in defining it in such a way as may leave some of the best and most beautiful buildings in the 'non' class while retaining some of the most dreadful ones within the fold. It is only by bettering the whole body of building that we shall be able to raise the summit.

And in America Frank Lloyd Wright spoke for many of the generation born around 1870 when he said that 'there is nothing more interesting or more important in this world today than trying to put into the houses in which our typical best citizens live something of the quality of a genuine work of art.' Sentiments such as Lethaby's and Wright's, when taken seriously (as they were in England), relegated the houses for the rich, which for centuries had made the running, into a backwater. Hou*sing* mattered more.

It is unlikely that these concerns occupied the night thoughts of Wright's English contemporary, Edwin Landseer Lutyens.* Ned Lutyens, 11th of 14 children, grew up in the depths of rural Surrey, among half-timbered cottages with huge mossy roofs, lost in vegetation, as in a Birkett Foster watercolour. Wandering the lanes on his bike (he was excused school on account of ill health), watching craftsmen at work, steeped in vernacular ways of building, his education, rarely for Englishmen of his class, was almost wholly visual rather than literate or numerate, and all his life he was to feel ill at ease in the sophisticated Oxbridge world into which his marriage to Lady Emily Lytton would propel him. His vulnerable nature attracted the affection of older women, by whom he was far more profoundly influenced than by the work of Ernest George and Peto, to whose Pont Street Dutch office he was apprenticed for a couple of years, and from which he escaped early, setting up in practice at the age of 20, with £100 capital, on the strength of one job. His heroes were Morris and Webb, but this first house, inevitably, was in the Old English manner of Norman Shaw.

---

*Title of Gertrude Jekyll's book of 1904.

*His father, ex-soldier and amateur painter, had been Landseer's favourite pupil.

Chief among those older women was the formidable, myopic, heart-of-gold gardener, Gertrude Jekyll, and it was in her woodland garden at Munstead that he built her home and his first truly characteristic house. Among my school-boy experiences of architecture was kneeling beside Ned Lutyens while he sketched on his knee the character and infinite possibilities of the classical Orders. But in 1896, when (aged 27) he built Munstead Wood, such possibilities were far from his mind. This deeply gabled house, built in golden Bargate stone, has something of Voysey in its long mullioned windows, but still more of Stokesay in the heavily timbered long gallery tucked in under its eaves. Here at last the Old English ideal is fully realised. To quote Miss Jekyll:

It is designed and built in the thorough and honest spirit of the good work of old days, and the body of it, so fashioned and reared, has as it were taken to itself the soul of a more ancient dwelling place. The house is not in any way a copy of any old building, though it emobodies the general characteristics of the older structures of its own district. Everything about it is strong and serviceable and looks and feels as if it would wear and endure forever.

For about ten years after Munstead Wood, Lutyens, always collaborating with Miss Jekyll on their garden settings, remained firmly in the romantic vernacular tradition. His practice grew rapidly, helped not only by his wife's connections but still more by the lavish coverage of his work in *Country Life*, the magazine founded by Edward Hudson in 1897. Deanery Garden, his lovely Tudoresque house for Hudson near the Thames at Sonning, has again the magic touch which none of his contemporaries in that mode could begin to match. You enter mysteriously through a hole in an ancient brick wall, then down a red and white vaulted undercroft with a cross-vista into a small courtyard, and so reach the double-height oak-beamed and orielled hall, which the beautifully balanced asymmetry of the whole design perfectly absorbs. Beyond, steps lead down and cross water into a garden fused with the house by the marriage of firm Lutyens geometry with soft Jekyll planting.

Tigbourne Court, by contrast, repeats the stone gables of Munstead Wood, with thin red bands of tiling to bring out the complex curved shape of the wings that embrace the triple gabled front – an essay in pure sculpture. Little Thakeham in Sussex has a symmetry of gables and an elegant oriel that the designer of Chastleton would have delighted in and that both

Concave wings and a Roman Doric porch lead into the gabled front of Lutyens's Tigbourne Court (1900). A band of red tiling is neatly run between the slim brick-mullioned windows and their simple entablatures. NEXT PAGES *Gledstone in West Yorkshire (1925-27) is Lutyens's last best house. The slim windows, kept away from the corners, give it a rather French look, while the portico is reminiscent of Webb's at The Vyne.*

Shaw and Voysey should have acknowledged as masterly – though there is no record that either ever did.

And so the brilliant successes accumulated, the houses growing larger as the Stock Exchange boom ushered in the golden Edwardian summer. In this process, inevitably, something was lost - the craftsman's touch which Morris had put his faith in. Lutyens could see what was at stake. 'In modern work [he writes in his revealing correspondence with Herbert Baker], unlike the old, the thinking machine is separated from the labour machine so that the modern architect has not the same absolutism as we gave the old men – where the thought and labour were from the same individual. This is where modern conditions must prevail, where they should tell. The thought and design in that they are specialised should become super-thought.' Super-thought, to him, could only mean the 'high game' of Classicism. 'In architecture, Palladio is the game!! It is so big – few appreciate it now, and it requires training to value and realise it. The way Wren handled it was marvellous . . . It is a game that never deceives . . . It means hard thought all through – if it is laboured it fails. There is no fluke that helps it – the very, what one might call, machinery of it makes it impossible except in the hands of a Jones or a Wren. . . . You cannot play originality with the Orders. They have to be so well digested that there is nothing but essence left.'

In 1905 he had the chance to build all this, landing a Bradford millionaire who was content to leave his architect an exceptionally free hand. So there stands, among Victorian villas in the Yorkshire commuter town of Ilkley, a stone Neo-classic villa called Heathcote, severe, meticulous, communing with itself, as might be in a similar street in Stuttgart. You cannot fault it, but you cannot love it. Now an office building, it stands as a lonely reminder of the axiom that, since the architect came on the scene, life is only ever breathed into houses by the meeting of two minds – or three!

It was a far cry from Munstead. On the defensive of his defiance of the *genius loci*, Lutyens made no bones about it: 'Would Wren (had he gone to Australia!) have burnt his knowledge and experience to produce a marsupial style – thought to reflect the character of her aborigines?' Lutyens never fell in love (as had Vanbrugh) with the North, and when he returned there, to great effect, after the Great War, he was too grand to interest himself in its powerful vernacular architecture. Meanwhile, he was soon back in the congenial south east, building for two bachelors at Sandwich a red brick country house in which the Queen Anne tradition at last loses its

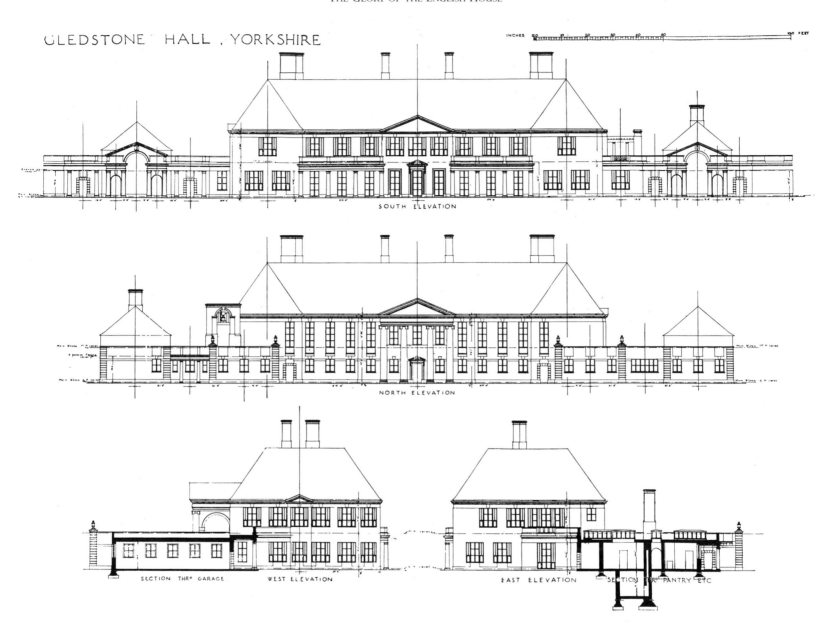

GLEDSTONE HALL, YORKSHIRE

SOUTH ELEVATION

NORTH ELEVATION

SECTION THRO GARAGE   WEST ELEVATION   EAST ELEVATION   SECTION THRO PANTRY ETC

*Lutyens's Gledstone elevations bring out the steep pitch of the main roof, compared
with the lodges and the little Doric loggias on the south front.*

quotation marks and reaches perfection. We have seen that Thackeray in
Kensington was the first to have a shot at it in the 1860s. Then, in 1873,
Wilfred Scawen-Blunt, poet and womaniser, built Crabbett Park in Sussex,
much closer to the originals, a complete anachronism at that date, and in-
cidentally the last great house to be designed by its owner and his wife. It
had no influence whatever, whereas the Salutation at Sandwich had an
enormous, uncountable progeny, as we shall see.

The Great War almost, but not quite, put paid to the story of the
English Country House: only a few of the very rich could thereafter afford
the cost of building and staffing one. One of them was the Skipton mill

owner Sir Amos Nelson, who had commissioned a local architect and then,
knowing nearby Heathcote, suggested he should collaborate with Lutyens.
Gledstone Hall (1925), the final result, lies in a shallow combe sloping to
the south and to a distant moorland horizon. The layout and landscaping
is wholly classical and very French (not a trace of Capability Brown), with
avenue approach, grand forecourt with twin lodges, and to the south a
central canal, with, on either side, two long stone piers or jetties thrusting
out into infinite space. (No doubt New Delhi, going on at the same time,
was in the architect's mind.) The pyramidal roofs of the lodges are deliberately less steep than the generous and unbroken hipped roof of the main

The garden front of the Salutation at Sandwich in Kent (1911) shows Lutyens speaking the Queen Anne language better than any of the late Victorians who had laid claim to it.

building, extravagantly covered in Cotswold stone. This great roof, and the tall, slim casement windows (cleverly kept well away from the corners of the wings) enhance the French effect; only the strong Ionic portico, reminiscent of John Webb's at The Vyne, is wholly English in feeling. Lutyens's magic touch is wholly unimpaired in this little masterpiece, now sadly shabby, yet once the most beautiful country house of the 20th century.

The age of domestic nostalgia that began in the 1860s, reached its creative apogee in the 1890s, and petered out in the shallows of the 1930s, coincided with an avalanche of ordinary house building for which there was no precedent in history. Inevitably the builders, and the anonymous designers who worked with them, picked up ideas from the dominant architects of that age, Norman Shaw and Lutyens. In some fields these were of real interest. The London Board School programme of the 1870s in which Stephenson played a leading part, and the architecture of the infant and idealistic London County Council around the turn of the century,

found simplified equivalents for the work of Shaw, Devey, and the arts and craftsmen; and similar influences inspired new settlements further afield like Bourneville and Wythenshawe. But eventually, when the speculative builders were given their head in 1930, half-timbered gables, leaded casements and wrought iron garden gates ended up in their world. This was the signal for the custom-built house to go neo-Georgian. A whole school of lesser men had grown up in the shadow of Lutyens, and very decent dull work they did – appropriate for neat housing estates, as at Hampstead Garden Suburb, Welwyn Garden City, and on the Duchy of Cornwall property in Lambeth, but not the stuff of which interesting architecture is made. For the better off, it was considered that a pediment, sash windows with some shutters, and a suitably tasteful door-case were all that was required. But 'Wrenaissance' (Lutyens's word) it was not. For, as it turned out, the Salutation was inimitable. As Kenneth Clark put it, 'perfection closes the door.'

PEEL YOUTH CLUB
ENTRANCE

PEEL CENTRE

CHAPTER 9

Futurism & Pastism

The Sun House in Hampstead (Maxwell Fry, 1935).

ONCE AGAIN, AS SO OFTEN IN THE PAST, THE TIME HAD COME to look abroad. The Continental scene was now infinitely more complicated than in the days of the Grand Tour. But there was one country which seemed to the neo-Georgians to offer a way forward. This was Sweden. Attracted to Stockholm by the fame of Ostberg's Town Hall, completed in 1923 – a late flowering of Arts and Crafts architecture more impressive than anything ours had achieved – architects found in Sweden an elegant if attenuated Neo-classicism which they could happily adopt for the Town Halls which were needed for all the new boroughs around London. For small houses too, Sweden offered a virtually astylar model, with low-pitch roofs, white walls, and wood casements, easily acclimatised, and eventually, translated into buff coloured brick and concrete tile, to become the Welfare State style of the first generation New Towns. One or two charming pre-war examples have survived.

But no sooner had this minor discovery been made than, in the Stockholm Exhibition of 1930, Sweden suddenly, overnight, went gracefully 'modern'. In the same year Le Corbusier's Villa Savoie appeared like something from outer space, on the flat fields outside Paris. The Modern Movement, as it was called, like most revolutions, was deeply rooted in the past, notably in French functionalism. Thus Durand in the early 19th century had written:

Public and private usefulness, and the happiness and preservation of mankind, are the aims of architecture. . . . Thus one should not strive to make a building pleasing, since if one concerns oneself solely with

PRECEDING PAGES *John Outram was perhaps the first architect since Lutyens to embrak seriously on enlarging the frontiers of classicism. This polychromatic house of 1986 is at Wadhurst in Sussex.* OPPOSITE *Lloyd Baker Street in London.*

A survivor of the early Modern Movement houses of the 1930s, Maxwell Fry's Miramonte on Kingston Hill, Surrey.

the fulfilment of practical requirements, it is impossible that it should not be pleasing.

And in 1860 Viollet le Duc, writing in the age of the great iron and glass masterpieces such as the Crystal Palace,

We reflect deeply on what we are doing and consult our reason only, without concerning ourselves about traditions or time-hallowed forms. . . . Ought we not in building rather to consider the complicated requirements of our civilisation than how to combine styles of architecture? . . . The nature of materials not employed formerly obliges us to employ new forms.

But mere functionalism would never have been enough. Again like most revolutions, modernism was highly romantic. The engineers were its heroes, with their lovely webs of steel and glass, their rugged, intensely masculine concrete, their huge spans. The dramatic exploitation of new materials was one strand of European modernism; it ran right through to our day in the work of architects like Norman Foster, Richard Rogers and Michael Hopkins. The first architect to think and design in terms of steel and glass was the German/American Mies van der Rohe, a perfectionist of classical severity and restraint. A small group of English houses followed in his footsteps.

The second strand was an attempt to escape from Edwardian vulgarity by reaching back once more to the original sources of western architecture in ancient Greece. Le Corbusier had the sunlight on the Parthenon in mind when he wrote that 'architecture is the masterly, correct, and magnificent play of masses brought together in light.' It was in the abstract geometry of great artefacts like grain silos and ocean liners that he saw the modern equivalent of that lost integrity. This gave a fresh sanction to monumental architecture in Rome and Paris (and later in Chandigarh and Brasilia), but it cut no ice in post-war Britain, dreaming of cottages.

The third strand derived from the work of Lutyens's great American contemporary, Frank Lloyd Wright. The typical Wright house had a rough masonry base, a spreading open-plan floor with the garden flowing in and out, and a wide sheltering roof – standing (in his words) 'dignified as a tree in the midst of nature'. Like Le Corbusier, he was a wizard with words. Here he speaks as an old man, in London, on the eve of war in 1939:

I declare that the time is here for architecture to recognize its own nature, to recognize that it is out of life itself for life as it is now lived – a humane and therefore an intensely human thing . . . to be lived in and to be lived in happily . . . It rejects all grandomania, every building that would stand in military fashion, heels together, eyes front, something on the right hand and something on the left. . . . Why then do you not trust life? Why does not great England on behalf of this great upward swing of life, on behalf of this desire to serve and interpret and develop humanity with fresh integrity; why does England not trust life?

In this 'naturism' modernism took its cue from Rousseau, from Morris, and from Lethaby – an eminently respectable heredity.

But not to the English. While in Paris in the 1920s all the arts blazed with excitement and adventure, London dozed, breathing the last enchantments of the British Empire, averting the eye from the strange forms which all over Europe, and most conspicuously in Germany, were emerging from the preaching of our own pundits. When some uncouth white boxes appeared on a hillside at Amersham, they were good for a laugh; modernism might be suitable for the odd factory, newspaper office, or yacht club, but not for the Englishman's home.

However, when in the 1930s many of the leaders of the modern movement suddenly landed in England, several of them as refugees, the thing had to be taken seriously. For what it put forward was a claim architecture had never made before, nothing less than the rescue of humanity from squalor, darkness and claustrophobia. For the generation that invented flight there seemed no limit to the freedom the new technology might confer. One could be (in Henry James' words) 'a man living in the open air of the world, indifferent to small considerations'. In Philip Johnson's glass house in the Connecticut woodlands there were no curtains; when darkness fell, floodlighting of the enclosing trees replaced them. Le Corbusier's two great books, *Vers Une Architecture* and *Une Ville Contemporaine*, appearing in English translation in 1927, had shown how this gift of light could be made available to everybody. The last revolution in English architecture, pioneered by Inigo Jones, had been an intellectual one: before the age of Romanticism there was no other way. This time the message could be conveyed in the language of poetry.

Those 20 or so pure white houses, dazzling in the Home Counties sunshine of that doomed decade, were soon blighted by depression and war. With their unprecedently thin walls, their vulnerable flat roofs, and corrodable steel windows, their chances of survival were poor anyway – perhaps even deliberately so, for a generation ago Sant Elia had written:

The fundamental characteristics of Futurist architecture will be expendability and transience. Our houses will last less time than we do, and every generation will have to make its own.

If this was a viable target, it was hit embarrassingly soon, not only for physical reasons, but for psychological ones. Neither our frail bodies nor our complex minds can take that much exposure. Our houses are not observatories; their job is first to shut out the excesses of nature, whether sun or rain or cold, and second to be store-houses of the lifetime's accumulations that protect our security and sense of identity. Inevitably, when the long war was over, most of the pioneer houses were done over to meet those needs, and turned into travesties of themselves. Only a handful survive unaltered, of which the best are Maxwell Fry's Sun House in Hampstead and the long low Miramonte he built near Kingston for one Jerry Brown.*

None of the white houses of the inter-war period were country houses in the old sense. Middleton Park in Oxfordshire, built for Lord Jersey by Lutyens and his son in 1937, was the last of them, and was scarcely used as such.** But just as the great houses and their estates were the scenario for

---

*Described thus in a letter to me:

''Ave you got them them plans, Mr Fry?' He regarded me I would say with something short of veneration. I produced the plans which he regarded dreamily as though discarding them in favour of new visions. 'First,' he said, 'the garridge. Rolls for me and a runabout for Miss Margaret (his pimply daughter), shuffer above. The rest of the 'ouse to scale and don't stint it Mr Fry. The best is good enough for Jerry Brown.'
The language could be that of many a Victorian client.

**That it had 12 bathrooms was a sign of what Christopher Hussey called the Cult of the Tub.

Farnley Hey in west Yorkshire (Peter Womersley, 1955), perched on the edge of a wooden ravine, is typical of its decade in the reaction to natural materials – rubble stonework, bricks and unpainted woodwork.

the architectural experiments of the European aristocracies of the 18th century, so the Modern House of the 20th century was the means by which European architects and their gallant clients made the canonical statements of the Modern Movement. Frank Lloyd Wright's ground-hugging prairie houses at one pole, Le Corbusier's airy *machines à habiter* at the other, and Mies van der Rohe's classic open plans on both sides of the Atlantic, were the icons of the avant-garde, just as in England Castle Howard and Chiswick House had once been. Of course the clients were no aristocracy. They had made their money in industry, trade and banking and they were the only private patrons modern art, modern music and modern architecture could get – as indeed they still are. In England of course, with the old county families beginning to sell up, there was such a prestigious alternative that only a few brave spirits, often of foreign or Jewish birth, took the risk of a modern house. Their aim, and their reward (to those who have experienced it) was a heightened sense of living, which was after all what modernism was all about.

For all this there was no urban equivalent. The Victorians had failed to match the Georgian terrace house: their urban architecture had been loftily contemptuous of its setting. And now the modernists' proper obsession was public housing and, inevitably, the flat. The small man, for whom the Class Three terrace houses had once been built, decamped to the urban fringes, where the speculators' golden harvest of the 1930s produced its miles and miles of semi-detached surburbia. It seemed in 1939 that the history of the English house as a work of urban art was over, like everything else one lived for.

It was not, of course. For the first decade after the war only housing and schools and some essential industrial/commercial work were allowed, but in the early 1950s, one by one, the first swallows of a new summer began to appear. There was no longer any need or desire for them to be revolutionary or eccentric. As its founders had intended, modernism had by now become the universal language of western architecture, as had classicism 200 years earlier. The insatiable need all over Europe for mass-produced housing, mass-produced schools and mass-produced office space had dictated this, and the interest of concerned architects was not in questions of style but in the need to combat monotony by ensuring that it was the components that were mass-produced rather than the buildings. They were themselves a new breed, emerging not from apprenticeship to famous names but from greatly expanded schools of architecture. The

A Cotswold garden house by Stout and Lichfield (1963) shows the continuing pre-dilection for local stone, and a more 'organic' approach to layout and silhouette.

senior people knew from experience that it was planning that had won the war and believed that it was planning alone that could moderate and humanise the rush of reconstruction.

The house itself had changed its physical nature over the last century or so. Although it had outgrown the desire to advertise the fact, it *was* a machine for living in, kept alive by a ganglion of tubes and cables of ever increasing complexity, yet as capable as a tree of benefiting by its micro-climate and occupying unaffectedly and gracefully its space in the world.

Designers could relax, now that the modern house was relieved of its role as manifesto. After six years of war, people had had enough of con-crete, and there was a yearning for natural materials, above all for stone, rubble walling and unpainted wood. Frank Lloyd Wright's sermon of 1939 could at last be attended to, and people sought to enfold their houses in Nature, rather than as in the past to stand out boldly from it. For Farnley Hey (1955), on the edge of a wooded ravine in West Yorkshire, Peter Womersley was able to get stone from a disused railway cutting nearby and

to line the open-plan, split-level interior with unrationed plywood. The outer walls are of stone or bricks to match it and dark vertical boarding – a mix of materials characteristic of the Festival style of the mid-50s. Peter Aldington's own house at Haddenham in Buckinghamshire is even more entwined in vegetation, in which the unaffected, freely composed, roughly plastered house with its widespread roofs modestly nestles, garden and house interwoven with consummate skill.

In those years the ordinary speculative builder could get his house types approved by planning committees without trouble, because they were so used to them, whereas architects of talent and originality were always obstructed. It was only after a long struggle, and through the support of the local community, that Stout and Lichfield were allowed to build in the jealously guarded Cotswolds, and only then perhaps because the house is invisible from anywhere. It lies amidst springs which the owner has har-nessed to create a secret, mossy, Japanese garden, with a little lake and watercourses entwining the free-shaped house, with its great wedge-

The SPAN *houses designed by Eric Lyons in the 1950s (these are in Blackheath)*
were a successful attempt to lure the middle classes out of suburban escapism into the
urban terraces of the London tradition.

shaped limestone walls. Both this house and Peter Aldington's were begun in 1963. The Aldingtons' took several years, since they built it with their own hands.

It was of course the low profile of these rural retreats that enabled them to bury themselves in vegetation. To demonstrate that the same effect could be achieved for the town dweller was the work of Eric Lyons, in the 1950s. After the decades of escapism from urban life into garden cities and semi-detached suburbia, it was an achievement to lure the middle-classes back into terrace houses at all, since they had by now become associated in the public mind with grimy Victorian inner cities or else with the decent, boring output of the Government's Housing Manuals. It was done by taking the housing off the street on to quiet backland, often already well planted, and then, at some loss of convenience, taking the cars away from the house fronts into garage courtyards. Windows could then peep out between the trees and shrubs of a richly planted garden, jointly maintained by owners' subscriptions. Elevations were generously glazed, painted

white, boarded, or tile hung, and roofs were flat – all as different as possible from council housing.

The flat roof, of course, unloved though it was, was absolutely necessary to the aesthetic of the early modern house, just as it had been to the architecture of Smythson and Burlington. It never had been very practical in our climate. An overnight snow storm had sent the gardeners up in frosty dawns to dig out the buried outlets behind the parapets, and if the thaw was too sudden a flood might descend on Adam's ceilings. In the houses of our century it survived the 1960s, but was then voted out by public opinion and changes of taste.

The high-minded, low-key, architecture of the 1950s was consistent with the most egalitarian period in English history. Neither could last. The battering ram which set off the assault on the quietest Scandanavian scene was brutally described as Brutalism – an adjective derived (as few realised) from one of Le Corbusier's statements: '*l'architecture, c'est avec des matières bruts établir des relations émouvantes*'.

This widely spreading house near Henley-on-Thames, by Francis Pollen (1965), built in London Stock bricks, shows the influence of Frank Lloyd Wright.

Its characteristic material, concrete, did make an appearance in private houses in the use of concrete blocks for internal walls, but by and large Brutalism passed domestic architecture by: there were soon so many other choices. They shaded of course into one another, but one can make some sense of the last 30 years by dividing them into three.

First, modernism flourished. The Modern House shed its capital letters and its pre-war Corbusian influences (partly because the master had shed them himself), but not the influence of the other two old masters of modernism, Frank Lloyd Wright and Mies van der Rohe. The ground-hugging, texture-loving Wrightian house is well exemplified by Francis Pollen's house of 1965 for his parents, hidden in a beechwood near Henley, with its wide eaves and tweedy yellow stock bricks. The wide spread of the house was widened still further by a charming little internal court and a wing with a separate studio/flat, so that its long horizontals contrast with the verticals of the surrounding beeches. The Miesian glass house survived too, a Cheshire cat of a house that in certain lights can vanish altogether: there is one in the churchyard at Dorchester, Oxford, which some have passed within a few yards without seeing. The example by Michael Hopkins, in a tightly built-up part of Hampstead, London, is remarkable for having, as far as can be seen from the street, no roof at all.

Secondly, there was neo-Georgian. Though he was not granted the wit*, the opportunities or the genius of Lutyens, one architect, Raymond Erith, soldiered on alone through the heyday of modernism, applying himself seriously and imaginatively to the English classical tradition, and ranging freely (but in reverse order) between Wrenish elaboration and the stripped classic of Henry Holland. He was a Suffolk man, and his best houses are in that region.

One can see an equally creative renewal of the tradition in the urban houses of a younger generation such as Colquhoun, Miller, and Jeremy Dixon. The former's semi-detached houses in Lanark Road, Hammersmith, London, speak the same straightforward language as those of the 1820s on the Lloyd Baker estate in Islington.

The rest of the neo-Georgian output of the last 30 years has ranged between correct and unimaginative pastiche and the builder's travesties that

*One must except from this generalisation his charming rebuild of Jack Straw's Castle on Hampstead Hill – alas under threat at the time of writing.

In total contrast is this glass house in Hampstead (Michael Hopkins, 1978), inspired
by the steel-and-glass purism of Mies van der Rohe.

tag along behind every fashion. To enthusiasts the word pastiche is an insult, since they believe that neo-Georgian is the return of the Prodigal Son to the God-given principles of Vitruvius. To sceptics it is just another costume from the fancy dress chest, and a pathetic symbol of English nostalgia and loss of nerve. The reader can take his choice.

Finally, there is Post-Modernism, which has come to be used as a portmanteau word for the fancy styles most easily studied on the speculative estates in London's Docklands. In its American origins in the work of Johnson, Moore and Venturi in the 1970s, Post-Modernism was a fun thing for ex-modernists, in which sly references to modernism and mannerist by-play with classical columns and cornices could both entertain the cognoscenti and please the populace. In England now, it has as wide a spread as neo-Georgian, from the monumental creations of serious architects like James Stirling and Terry Farrell at one end of the scale to the silliest speculators' pseudo-Victoriana at the other. The most articulate, if also the most eccentric, of the serious Post-Modernists is John Outram.

Not for him Venturi's use of Corinthian bits and pieces as a form of decoration; for him, as for George Dance in the early 1800s, a column is a column, a thing for carrying loads, or anyway pretending to, and he likes to emphasise its monumentality in an almost Cyclopean manner. He loves he says, the rhetorical potential of classicism, its 'vulgar side, the bright colours, the garbled and chaotic iconography, the esotericism and eroticism. All these things came tumbling out of the classical and medieval cupboard once it had been unlocked by the permissive '60s'. 'Tactile values', he believes, got lost in modernism which 'in freezing the psyche, robbed it of lodging and sustenance'.

The New House, designed by Outram for a Swedish industrialist and his wife and built in 1986, sits on the elevated site of an old one in Sussex, and surveys a wide stretch of parkland occupied by vast herds of deer. The building is one-storey, steel-framed, H-shaped, and incorporates the 19th-century Gothic walls of the old conservatory; but these bare facts say nothing about this house, for, to begin with, it bears no resemblance to

*A group of semi-detached houses in Hammersmith, London, designed by Colquhoun
and Miller in the 1980s, is closely related to the houses built on the Lloyd Baker
estate in Islington in the 1820s (shown on page 190).*

any other. Its geometric polychromy is like the marble lining of a Byzantine church. Even to list its facing materials – terrazzo in a variety of colours, stripes and blocks, fat red brick columns, black bricks, patterned marbled pavings, trellises, veneers – is merely bewildering. The segmental roofs and the shallow internal vaults faintly echo Soane's breakfast parlour at No 13 Lincoln's Inn Fields, the trellis doors his breakfast room at No 12; and in its polychromy and its joyous escape from conventional and classical detail it gives an inkling of what, were he alive today, Soane might be up to. Here fashion folds its tents and slinks away, for the house is (I hope) inimitable and, perhaps, a minor masterpiece.

One of these days, no doubt, after this rich diet, we are in for a dose of English puritanism. Already, one or two architects, sick of styles, are burying houses under the ground – Man as Rabbit. It is not for the photographer, nor the writer, nor the prophet, to follow them there.

201

CHAPTER 10

Retrospect

Basildon Park, Berkshire.

I N THE LITTLE SPECK OF TIME AND SPACE THAT IS ENGLISH history, the glory of the English house emerged in the 15th century and faded in the 20th. Its four great centuries – from 1514 to 1914 to be precise – lasted as long as most of the great ages of culture and civilisation. Like all the others it rested, of course, if not on slavery, on privilege, on comparative peace, and on the enormous wealth of a small minority. But in England this was more widely diffused than in other comparable societies. The glory shone on thousands of modest houses of the middling sort – on manor houses and rectories, on merchant's houses in the country towns, and on the terraces, squares and crescents of the cities and resorts. One cannot even deny it to the masons' soundly built villages of the northern dales and the limestone belt, or the carpenters' rugged oak of East Anglia, the Weald of Kent, and the Welsh Marches. It is not at all easy to draw a line between the great house, the nice house, and the cottage.

But lines can be drawn – have drawn themselves – across the story as it has unfolded. Political insecurity, wars or rumours of wars always discourage building, and their incidence divides the story into four, which we roughly equate with the centuries, and roughly label Tudor/Jacobean, Restoration, Georgian, and Victorian. Their boundaries, defined only approximately by wars and reigns, are indistinct in terms of dates, because designing and building spreads over several years, and provincial builders were always way behind London. But they are conspicuously distinct in character, and consequently in the affections of many people. Indeed, the attitudes of succeeding generations to these four great legacies is a clue in itself to the history of taste.

PRECEDING PAGES *Cothay Manor, Somerset.* OPPOSITE *Stokesay Castle, Shropshire.*

Loseley Park, Surrey.

Each generation, of course, is contemptuous of the work of the one before, and often of the one before that. In the present 1990s, people are only just coming round to the work of the 1950s. They are contemptuous not only of what their immediate predecessors did, but of what they thought. Thus the neo-Georgians of the 1920s and 1930s found it difficult to enjoy Tudor architecture because their parents and grandparents had loved it, over-restored it, and imitated it. 'Barbarism' was the view of Tudor architecture taken by George Chapman, the translator of Homer (though he was a late Elizabethan himself), and we have noted what Charles Dickens thought of the late Georgian London in which he got a

job as a boy. But the Victorians loved Queen Anne, just as the Jacobeans loved the medieval, whether barbaric or not, and just as we have come round to enjoying what used to be thought of as the vulgarity of the Edwardians. But the four great centuries are now all of them remote enough for us to stop the pendulum of taste and take a more detached view of each one.

'There was a star danced, and under that I was born.' The Elizabethan age had 'a peculiar radiance,' wrote Harold Nicolson, 'not seen in Europe since the lost glamour of fifth-century Greece'. The release from the re-ligious conflicts that still infected France, the idolisation of the young

The staircase at Sudbury Hall, Derbyshire.

Queen, the emergence out of feudalism of the most open society in Europe, the defeat of the Armada, the opening up of the globe – all these escapes created the exhilaration which Shakespeare puts into the mouth of Henry V. These people would enjoy fashion but never be enslaved by it. 'Dear Kate,' says Henry to his French wife, 'you and I cannot be confined within the weak list of a country's fashion. We are the makers of manners, Kate.' So one should not take Elizabethan architecture too solemnly: it was an adventure and it was full of contradictions. It was the most derivative since the 12th century (and, as before, from France), yet at the same time the most emancipated. It took on board every latest Renaissance fashion,

yet never wished to shed its late medieval, Perpendicular attachments. It expressed itself, for the first time in England, not in churches but in palaces and country houses, and these were built not by the Queen nor by the old landed aristocracy, but by a new class of clever and ingenious men whom she had sought out and enriched. Yet the epitome of these strange, contradictory houses was built by a woman, exploiting aristocratic wealth.

One has to return to Hardwick, most miraculous and most mysterious of survivors, rational on plan, yet when you go inside it seems all improvisation and serendipity; darkly sinister in silhouette, yet when you go inside it is a blaze of light; it seems in the end as unfathomable as the

Hawkstone Hall, Shropshire.

personality of Shakespeare himself, who published *Richard* II in the year that old Bess moved in.

Those who fall under the spell of houses such as this will dispute the conventional, heroic view of Inigo Jones as the pioneer in England of the Great Game. They will contrast the wild, fabulous plasterwork of Hardwick and Haddon, in manner and mythology rooted in English life, with the boring Italian *putti* and insipid Grecian goddesses of the imported Renaissance; they will compare the fiercely idiosyncratic hall at Hardwick with Jones's cold cube at Greenwich, with its heavily Roman ceiling. They will cast Inigo Jones as the master-mind of a *dirigiste* coup that failed, and the survival of 'Englishness' right through the 17th century as a popular triumph.

From the century that separates Compton Wynyates from Blickling it is natural to pick out the reign of Elizabeth as its apogee; but art can never be so confined. The real limits of that prolific age were imposed by the religious conflicts and violence with which it began and ended. Its ending,

the Civil War, also defines the Restoration, that comparatively short period in which what we now call the Georgian house was born. It is often called the Age of Wren, but in fact the great house as it emerged out of the War was not Wren-like at all. The trouble is that the finest of these earliest Restoration houses, Clarendon and Coleshill, are no more. Regular leaded casements in cross-shaped mullions, hipped roof with dormer windows, central cupola, 'Captain's Walk': we find each feature either at Ashdown or at Belton, but the first, magical though it is, is a miniature, and the second, handsome though it is, is too late and too obviously taken from Clarendon to have the freshness of an original work of art.

Internally, the mystery, the sense of roots, deep in the 'dark backward and abysm of time', has been totally dispelled. How should it not have been, in the age of Newton? But there is still a transitional ambiguity in these houses. The chunky and often fanciful oaken staircase balustrades look back to the 16th century, but on the other hand the Long Gallery, that great English amenity, has had to go. As Adam was to find at Syon, the

Stourhead, Wiltshire.

shape was an impossible one to adapt to the proportions of a classical interior. The same applies to the small oak panels on the parlour walls: the dado rail has come in, and above it the Knellers and Lelys fit comfortably into large panels symmetrically adjusted to the length of the wall. It is all, now, very sensible. Both painters had been brought over from the Netherlands, in an age in which England was closely involved with the young republic in the build-up of the Protestant alliance against Louis XIV. Eltham, with its red brick, pilasters and pediment, forbear of so many such houses, is a transcription of the Mauritzhuis at the Hague. For the moment the grand manner, and with it the influence of the numinous Roman allusions of France and Italy, seemed to have deserted English domestic architecture.

But it was only a moment, for the first year of the new century saw the building of Castle Howard, and with it the dawn of what conventional 20th-century opinion has seen as the heroic century of English domestic architecture. Certainly the age had its heroes, living and dead, and with

the arrival on the scene of Taste, of the Grand Tour, and of fashionable impatience with the *démodé*, there was more scope for them than ever before. But all this excitement took place against a backcloth of extraordinary consistency, even standardisation (much disliked by the Victorians, much admired by housing architects of the 20th century). The Georgian refacing in the main streets of all our towns, and beyond them the new terraces, squares and crescents with their endless rows of front doors – all done by self-made speculative builders working for landowner/developers – this was as important an architectural achievement, affecting far more people, as any of the adventures of the rich.

Equally standardised all through the century was the Georgian box, whether it was the professional man's suburban retreat, the new rectory, or the rebuilt manor house, and of course from this familiar base (central doorcase, five windows above) the pyramid of grandeur, always symmetrical, rises without a break to the palatial frontages of Wentworth Woodhouse and Stowe.

Fitzroy Square, London.

At that high level, the whole age could be said to be steeped in Romanticism, if by that word we mean an art that is concerned with associations and evocations rather than pure form. Yet, as with all such generalisations, we would have to except outstanding individualists – Hawksmoor at the beginning and Soane at the end. Vanbrugh, for example, with his love of silhouettes and obsession with castles, was a born Romantic. And so were the Palladians who, despite their severity and formalism, lived in a dream of Ancient Rome as profound as any Victorian Goth's dream of the Middle Ages. And the gardens and parks in which they sat their great houses were perhaps the most romantic, as they were certainly the most uniquely English, creation of the 18th century.

When, with Nash and Repton, Romanticism shaded into the Picturesque it shed its solemnity, achieving during the Regency a lightness of touch not seen before or since, until this was overborne by the scholarly but stodgy Grecians, followed by the high-minded Goths. Unfortunately neither of these parties, to begin with, could muster an architect of genius. Of the serious Goths, Pugin, that master of the interior *mis-en-scène*, never had, indeed seems to have despised, the compositional skills of the born architect, whereas his contemporary Butterfield, who had them, was not

Sezincote, Gloucestershire.

equipped by nature to take any interest in the domestic interior. Visual confusion had taken the place of clarity.

We are among the Victorians, of whom it must be said that if the 17th century was an age of contradictions, still more so was the 19th. This is the first age which, despite its recent rehabilitation, even its most passionate admirers admit did as much harm as good. The overriding cause was not so much aesthetic as economic – the effect of coal and iron industrialisation, population explosion and unprecedented wealth. Every architect worth his salt had rather (in principle) do a dozen really good buildings than a hundred mediocre ones. But whereas Vanbrugh designed only seven country houses from scratch, Archer five, Campbell eight, Burlington four, and Robert Adam none, the Scottish architect William Burn, who flourished in the middle years of the 19th century, built no less than 60 country houses from scratch, many of them very large, and made substantial alterations to another 140.* As for the cities and towns, the explosive demand for new accommodation was not within the concern, and quite beyond the competence, of the Victorian architect.

*These figures are approximate, depending on attribution and documentation.

West Wycombe Park, Buckinghamshire.

What made the huge output of Burn, Barry and Salvin less boring for them and more enjoyable for us, was their readiness to do you a design in any style you chose. This adaptability, pioneered by James Wyatt, survived well into the 20th century. They had their preferences, of course, and it was when they were given full rein by a client ready to enter fully into the spirit of the thing that they produced their most spectacular work. Thus it was that, despite their huge practices, Salvin at Harlaxton, at the outset of the period, and Norman Shaw at Cragside towards its end, could still summon up great reserves of energy and imagination.

Energy, this was their secret – an energy that makes the architects of the previous century look like dilettantes, which indeed several of them were. This energy was not just that of the architects, who produced their enormous output without electricity, without typewriters, travelling by horse and buggy along country lanes to sites miles from the nearest station; it was also that of the craftsmen and labourers, whose workmanship, all achieved with medieval equipment, still astonishes us, with all our hardware. On the other hand, whereas the 18th-century architects and amateurs were men of the world, Europeans, a part of the Enlightenment, most of the Victorians were blinkered provincials who were simply not interested in what was going on across the Channel – a condition in which British architects were to remain until the 1930s. They should not take the blame for this. Waterloo had seen the defeat not just of Napoleon but of all universalist ideals. From then on each nation-state felt free to do its own thing, good or bad.

Even William Morris and the aesthetes of the Rossetti circle who led the attack on the stuffy old High Victorians were themselves provincial in that sense. But there was this difference: that the comparatively modest 'Old English' and 'Queen Anne' houses done by the Devey/Shaw/Nesfield generation were admired and imitated abroad, particularly in Germany and New England, whereas the great mansions of the High Victorians were ignored.

Lutyens, bridging the centuries, achieved two remarkable things. In his youth he 'purified the language of the tribe': Old English and Queen Anne, in his hands, ceased to be parodies of the originals. And in his middle age he became one of the very few English architects (the others were Hawksmoor, Vanbrugh and Soane) to revitalise classical architecture by giving it a completely original stamp of his own. But the one thing he failed to recreate from the past was the great urban tradition that had run

Alton Castle, Staffordshire.

to seed in the mid-19th century. Almost all his urban buildings, and particularly his houses for the rich, are too big for their style.

Apart from this, the country house, in its old sense and as a glorious subject for experiment, virtually ceased to exist in the first half of the 20th century. In *The Book of the Modern House* edited by Patrick Abercrombie and published on the eve of World War II, examples are classified, *inter alia*, as Country Houses, Town Houses, and Suburban Houses, but really they are all alike, sub-Georgian or sub-Cotswold, with sashes and shutters or Crittall steel windows, garage, and half a dozen low ceilinged rooms inside – all perfectly decent and done by reputable architects. The Modern House,

newly landed, has a small section to itself, written up by Oliver Hill, who could do you one if you were ready to risk it – a flexible man, like William Burn.

Plainly the 'glory' has departed: we do not have, or are not supposed to have, the people to sustain it, either the masters or the servants. No cause for nostalgia: small can be beautiful. Most modern houses outside London, if they get the space for it, are one-storey (*never* bungalows!), although in the case of the Modern House this may be hoisted up on stilts. So they cannot aspire, and have no desire, to dominate a landscape, but rather, in the Picturesque mode, to merge with it. If it is uneven, or better still

House at Pen Pits, *a painting by Edward Wadsworth, 1936.*

rocky, they revel in split levels, uneven ceiling heights, clerestory lighting – easily achieved when you have the roof to play with. These predilections go back to the open plan, which came in with central heating as a way to give character to a very limited amount of floor space. All this is not only irrespective of style, excluding only, and obviously, the neo-Georgian; it prefers to ignore the concept of style, even though the designer knows that history will not. The site, the microclimate, the client's needs, these are the generators.

Rather than being an experiment in style, as in the past, the one-off house offers an experiment in life-style to those who desire it and can afford it – an adventure to which one can set no limits and predict no outcomes. Who knows? Perhaps the Great House will make a come-back, accommodating a reaction to the extended family or a fashion for community living. Redundant farmhouses and the empty hearts of ruined parks will offer themselves as sites. All we can be sure of is that what will happen will be the last thing we expect.

A Note on Books

Of general architectural histories concerning the story told in this book the most authoritative and readable are *Architecture in Britain 1530-1830* by John Summerson (1953), in the Pelican History of Art, and *Victorian Architecture* by James Stevens Curl (1990). H. M. Colvin's *Biographical Dictionary of English Architects 1660-1840* (1954) is an invaluable reference book.

The first systematic and fully illustrated *History of the English House* was Nathaniel Lloyd's great tome of 1931. On a smaller scale, Hugh Braun's *The Story of the English House* (1940) is useful for the first two centuries, as is Reginald Turner's *The Smaller English House* (1952) for the first three. *The National Trust Book of the English House* (1985) by Clive Aslet and Alan Powers is the most recent and comprehensive of the shorter histories.

On the great country houses the pioneer work was done by the publishers *Country Life* early this century, leading to Christopher Hussey's three-volume *English Country Houses 1714-1840* (1951-3), and carried forward by Mark Girouard's *The Victorian Country House* (1971). There is as yet no survey of equivalent authority for the 20th century, though *The Book of the Modern House*, edited by Patrick Abercrombie, sums up the state of things in 1939 and *The Last Country Houses*, by John Martin Robinson, does the same for the neo-Georgians in 1988. The best short history of the country house is still Olive Cook's of 1974, handsomely illustrated by A. F. Kersting's photographs.

For town houses Summerson's *Georgian London* (1988) is essential.

Walter Ison's *The Georgian Buildings of Bath* (1948) and Andrew Byrne's *London's Georgian Houses* (1986) are also useful.

Of the many books on particular periods, Girouard's *Robert Smythson* (1961) is important for the Elizabethan age, and I have enjoyed James Lees-Milne's books on *The Tudor Renaissance* (1951), on *The Age of Adam* (1947), and on the Palladian *Earls of Creation* (1962). For *The Greek Revival* there is J. Mordaunt Crook (1972), and for *The Gothic Revival* Kenneth Clark's pioneer study first published in 1928, reissued in 1962. Dr Crook's *The Dilemma of Style* (1987) illuminates the 'Style Wars' of the 19th and 20th centuries.

There are many monographs on individual architects, among them *Inigo Jones* (Summerson, 1966) *Hawksmoor* and *Vanbrugh* (Kerry Downes, 1959 & 1987), *Kent* (Michael Wilson, 1984), *Archer* (Marcus Whiffen, 1950), *Soane* (Dorothy Stroud, 1961), *Nash* (Terence Davis, 1960), *Robert Adam* (Alistair Rowan, 1990), *Holland* (Stroud, 1950), *A. W. Pugin* (Trappes-Lomax 1932), and *Norman Shaw* (Arthur Bloomfield, 1940). The best book on *Lutyens* is still Hussey's memorial biography of 1950.

Osbert Lancaster's wicked cartoons in *Pillar to Post* (1938) and *Homes Sweet Homes* (1939) should be studied after (but not before) you have read this book.

Finally, for particular places, never fail to consult Pevsner's magisterial and witty county guides to *The Buildings of England*, an achievement as remarkable as the houses themselves.

OPPOSITE *Castle Howard at sunset.*

Glossary

ARCADE   Series of arches supported by columns or by flat-sided piers

ARCHITRAVE   Moulded frame of a door or window

BALUSTRADE   A series of balusters supporting a handrail or coping, the whole either of wood, stone or metal

BARGEBOARD   A board fixed below the eaves of a gable to protect the rafters

BASTION   Projection from the main wall of a fortress to enable a garrison to cover the adjacent walls

BATTLEMENT   Parapet at roof level with gaps or crenellations for archers to shoot through

BAYS   Divisions of an elevation defined by vertical features

BUTTRESS   Vertical or sloping projection from a wall to give it support

CAME   Lead strip supporting small panes of glass

CAMPANILE   A bell-tower

CANTILEVER   Horizontal projection supported by a downward force behind a fulcrum consisting of a wall or column

CASEMENT   Window hinged at the side

CLERESTORY   High-level series of windows immediately below a roof

CLUNCH   Chalk used as a building material

COLONNADE   Series of columns supporting a beam or classical entablature (qv)

COLONNETTE   A miniature column

COMPOSITE   (see Orders)

CORINTHIAN   (see Orders)

CORNICE   Moulded projection along the top of a wall. In classical architecture, the topmost member of an entablature

COTTAGE ORNÉ   (French)   A deliberately picturesque cottage

COVE   A concave moulding. A coved ceiling is curved downwards to meet the wall

CRENELLATION   (see Battlement)

CUPOLA   A small dome

DADO   Protective, sometimes panelled, finish along the lower part of an interior wall

DORMER   A window projecting from the slope of a roof

EAVES   Overhanging edge of a roof

ELEVATION   Any side of a building, or a scale drawing of it

EMBRASURE   A small space or opening created out of the thickness of a wall

ENTABLATURE   Collective name for the three horizontal components (cornice, frieze, architrave) carried by a wall or by columns

FACADE   Any face of a building

FENESTRATION   The arrangement of windows in a building

FINIAL   A pointed skyline ornament

FRIEZE   A horizontal band of ornament or sculpture, generally below a ceiling

GABLE   The triangular area of a wall at the end of a pitched (sloping) roof

GAZEBO   A raised summer house commanding a view

HIPPED ROOF   A roof with sloping instead of gabled ends

INGLENOOK   A small seat contrived in the corner of a large open fireplace

KEYSTONE   Central stone at the apex of an arch, without which it would collapse

LATTICE   A pattern formed of straight interlaced lines

LINENFOLD   Tudor panelling when each panel is carved to represent a piece of vertically folded linen

LOGGIA   An open, generally colonnaded, gallery built against the outside wall of a building

MANNERIST   A style of architecture, generally classical, in which conventional features are used in an unconventional way

MULLION   Vertical member dividing the lights in a window opening

NEO-CLASSIC   A style of architecture derived directly from Greek or Roman examples rather than from Renaissance versions

NICHE   Vertical recess in a wall, generally intended for a statue

NOGGING   Bricks used to fill the spaces between wall timbers in a timber-framed building

ORDERS   Rules of design and proportion, applied originally to the three classical Greek combinations of column and entablatures (qv) – the Doric, Ionic and Corinthian. In Roman and later times hybrids were developed such as the Composite, which combines Ionic and Corinthian features

ORIEL   A window projected from the main wall surface

OEIL DE BOEUF   (French)   An oval window or opening

PARAPET   A protective wall along the edge of a roof or other dangerous drop

PARGETER   A plasterer specialising in moulded or incised decoration of an external wall surface

PARTERRE (French)   A formal garden laid out in geometrical patterns.

PAVILION   A garden house or terminal building at the ends of the wings of a classical mansion

PEDIMENT   Originally the triangular gable end of a Greek temple; later used ornamentally as the central feature of a classical elevation or over doorways and windows

PERGOLA   A simplified double arcade, generally unroofed, used as a garden feature

PERISTYLE   A range of columns surrounding the external walls or central court of a classical building

PERPENDICULAR   The latest of the three historic periods of English medieval architecture, beginning in the late 14th century

PIANO NOBILE (Italian)   The principal floor of a classical building, generally with a ground-level basement beneath it

PIER   Large masonry support for an arch or lintel

PILASTER   A classical column attached ornamentally to a wall, or a flat projection representing it

PORTE-COCHÈRE (French)   A projected porch large enough to shelter carriages halting at a front door

PORTICO   A classical temple front, generally with a pediment (*qv*), and generally the central feature of a main elevation

QUADRANT   A quarter circle

QUOINS   Dressed stones at the angles of a building, alternately long and short

RAGSTONE   A rough limestone found in the Weald of Kent

RESTORATION   The period following the return of the monarchy in 1660

RUSTICATION   Treatment of a stone wall to give an impression of massiveness, either by recessed joints or by roughening of the surface or both

SASH WINDOW   Opening lights which slide vertically by means of cords and counterweights

SCAGLIOLA   A polished composition surface in imitation of marble, generally used for the shafts of columns

STUCCO   A fine lime plastered surface used externally and often painted

STUDS   The vertical components in a timber-framed building

TROMPE L'OEIL (French)   A wall or ceiling painted to give an illusion of depth or distance

TRUSS   A timber framework placed at intervals across a building to carry the beams ('purlins') which in turn support the common rafters

TUSCAN   A Roman version of the Doric order

UNDERCROFT   A vaulted space supporting a main floor

VERANDAH   A wide shelter built against an external wall and supported by columns or posts (American: 'porch')

VOLUTE   Spiral 'ears' at the corners of an Ionic capital

VOUSSOIRS   Wedged-shaped stones round the edge of an arch

Index

Figures in italics refer to illustrations

ACKNOWLEDGEMENTS

The publishers are grateful to the following individuals or institutions for supplying illustrations or allowing them to be reproduced: Peter Aprahamian, 144; Architectural Press, 191; British Architectural Library, Royal Institute of British Architects, 83, 127, 139 bottom, 154, 169, 170; Castle Howard Collection, 84; Alison Coker, 181; Country Life Library, 37, 97, 99 bottom, 205; Viscount Esher, 30, 139 top; Fotomas Index, 57; A.F. Kersting, 105; Mansell Collection, 113; National Trust Photographic Library, 13, 67; The Earl of Pembroke/David Miller, 60; Victoria & Albert Museum/Alex Starkey, 151; Victoria Art Gallery, Bath City Council, 109.